Bright Ideas
Display

Written by
Rhona Whiteford and Jim Fitzsimmons

Contents

Published by Scholastic Publications Ltd,
Marlborough House, Holly Walk,
Leamington Spa, Warwickshire CV32 4LS.

© 1988 Scholastic Publications Ltd

Reprinted in 1989
Written by Rhona Whiteford and
Jim Fitzsimmons
Edited by Jackie Cunningham-Craig
Sub-edited by Jane Morgan
Illustrations by Gay Galsworthy

Printed in Great Britain by
Loxley Brothers Ltd, Sheffield

ISBN 0 590 70950 X

Front and back cover: designed by Sue Limb,
Photographs by Martyn Chillmaid.

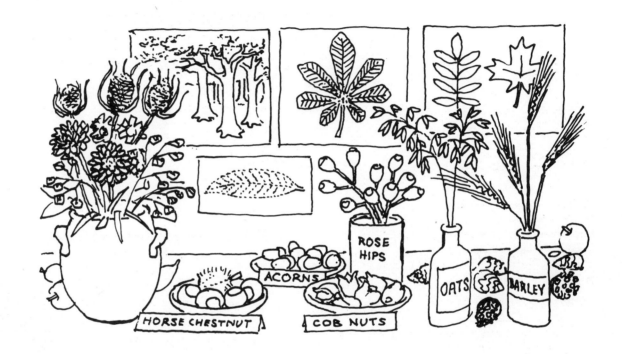

Introduction

Teachers are under a great deal of pressure in the busy school day, and some feel that they haven't got time for display or that it is simply not worth the effort. However, concern for the environment has never been greater and display plays a vitally important part in the education of our children. The conditions and surroundings in which we live have a tremendous effect on our mood, efficiency and attitudes, and we owe it to ourselves and the children to make the very best of what we have.

Every teacher knows the thrilled reaction of children to strange new things imaginatively displayed. Such stimulating visual experiences can help to develop aesthetic sensibilities whilst extending general knowledge. New points of interest can form the basis of much thought, speech and expression in various media, such as poetry, drawing, painting and modelling, as well as more research into the subject, and possibly a scientific study.

Display is used to provide stimulus, set an example and show children's work off to its best advantage to be admired. There are times, however when work which may be a child's best effort, needs to be well presented to be properly appreciated by all. Having said that, even a masterpiece will look better if it is displayed attractively.

If you feel that you haven't a flare for display, don't worry. It is true that some people have a gift for selecting colour, line, shape, and so on, but all of us can learn through trial and error to develop an idea of what is best for the purpose and occasion. What you do need is the ability to be inventive, to adapt ideas to suit your own purpose. Be on the look-out for display ideas in other classrooms, schools, shops, exhibitions and on television. You may spot a colour, shape or textural idea which is just right for your current topic. Collect trifles and unusual odds and ends to make a display store (see page 35), and above all be open to suggestion.

The children can and should be involved in most display work around school, particularly in the discussion stage, when they can be part of the exchange of ideas and the decision-making. Neatness and attention to the detail of layout are part of good practice in all children's work, and the craftsmanship involved in the mounting and presentation of work for displays can be taught from infants onwards.

It is vitally important that the teacher draws the children's attention to displays around school, so that they will learn to observe as well as be involved in their own environment and, not least, be appreciative of others' efforts. Above all, display is a teaching aid, and there should be one or two items which can be handled and many that contain children's work.

Rhona Whiteford
Jim Fitzsimmons

Techniques

Display in the primary school often reflects the interests of the children at a given time, this may be connected to any aspect of the curriculum such as a seasonal display of topic work.

Drawings, paintings, prints or rubbings, together with written work, are usually presented as 2-D displays, but models, constructions, man-made or natural objects require different display techniques because of their 3-D nature.

All work which is to be mounted for display needs to be considered in the following ways; the materials chosen, the colours selected and the method of mounting to be used.

An untrimmed, unmounted, unlabelled piece of work fixed by a drawing pin does not give the impression of a caring teacher.

Choosing colours

Since bright colours or brightly patterned backgrounds tend to detract from the work to be displayed, it is best to use neutral colours, such as pale blue, grey, fawn, black and white. Wherever possible, the colour for the mount should pick up one of the colours in the piece of work. This often works much better than a colour contrast as it provides a good balance for the display. It is a good idea to consider the overall colour effect when starting any display.

Hot colours

For a fire or flame effect: crimson, scarlet, red, vermilion, orange, gold.

Warm colours

For autumn or a sunset: red, vermilion, orange, rust, amber, ochre, yellow, lemon.

Cool colours

For ice, rain or winter: turquoise, aquamarine, blue, ultramarine, purple, lavender, lilac.

Rich colours

For royal themes or pirates or treasure: purples, lavender, mauve, magenta, crimson, red, pink, gold.

Mounting the work

Single mounting

Work which has had all the rough edges trimmed off is then stuck on to a suitable background: eg dark on light or light on dark. A better effect is achieved if the lower margin is larger than the top and a thin line is drawn round the work with a black felt-tipped pen.

Double mounting

Follow the same procedure as for single mounting and then put the work on to a second background of a different colour, tone or texture. This second background may also be of a different shape.

Window mounting

Cut a window out of a piece of card and stick the piece of work on to the back of the card so that it shows through the window.

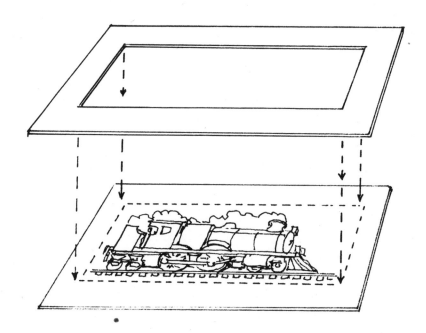

Frame mounting

More substantial frames can be made from wood or strong card. The construction is similar to the window-frame technique but a backing sheet is attached with one side left open so that the piece of work may be inserted. The frame can be reused several times.

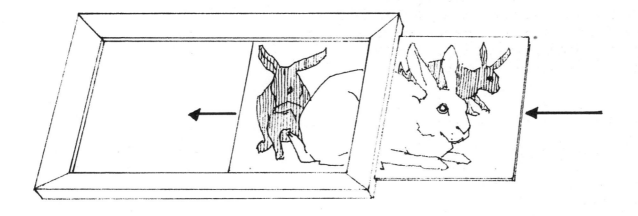

Single or double mounted 2-D work can be displayed
flat or in a variety of 3-D ways.

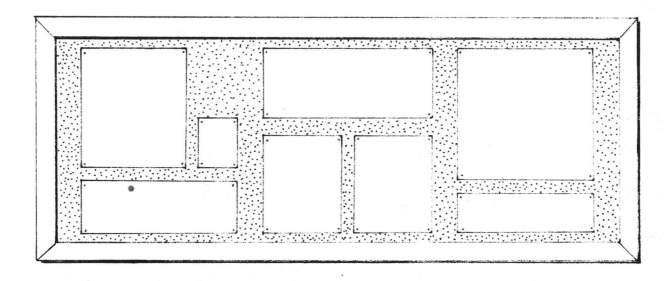

Shapes of mounting

The shape of mounts can add to the effectiveness of a display. A simple way of making written work stand out is by mounting it on a circle, rectangle or any other shape cut out of black paper. Placing the piece of work a few centimetres to the left or the right, up or down, will make the piece of work look 3-D.

When the colouring is completed, mount one circle on top of the other with the shading placed on opposite sides.

Another exciting way to display circles of work is to use a double mounting technique. This creates the effect of a sphere with a hole in it. For each piece of work you will need two paper or card circles cut to different sizes. The children should colour half of each circle in solid shading or in a wheel spoke technique, lines of colour spreading out from the centre.

Prepare the written work by cutting it into a circle. Use a pair of compasses to draw a circle round the piece of work, leaving a plain border round the edge. The depth of this border will depend on the size of the work. You can cut the mounting paper into a circle before giving it to the children. Draw a circle within this as your border. Using a stencil, top infants onwards can do this themselves. Older juniors can use a pair of compasses.

Once completed, the work can be mounted either concentrically or off-centre.

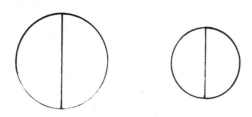

Another way of creating a 3-D effect is to mount a piece of work on to backing paper as shown. Make the left and top sides the same width, say 2 cm, and the right and bottom side much wider, say 6 cm. Cut off the opposite wide corners at an angle of 45°.

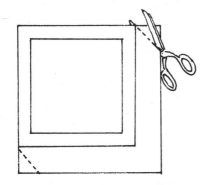

Repeat for each piece of work and mount them in a group.

Depth can be achieved in a similar way with circles, hexagons and other shapes.

A frieze
A very popular way of displaying children's work is to make a frieze, using a roll of sugar-paper as a backing sheet. If the subject matter allows, the frieze should be built up in stages. Suitable subjects are historical scenes and different landscapes, such as nature, geography, space and underwater.

A street scene could be built up in the following way. The elements of the frieze are drawn by the children on cartridge or drawing-paper and cut out, leaving a thin border all round. The various horizons should be indicated on the roll of frieze paper, starting with the houses and other buildings. Then outline the area of the roadway and place the vehicles in various positions, some overlapping the outlines of the buildings to create depth. Finally, the figures walking on the pavement may be placed on the frieze, again overlapping some of the vehicles. The size of the figures at the front should be larger than those at the back of the frieze according to the perspective required.

3-D effects

Art work or written work, single or double mounted, may be folded down the middle like a book and then pinned or stapled to the wall or display-board as shown.

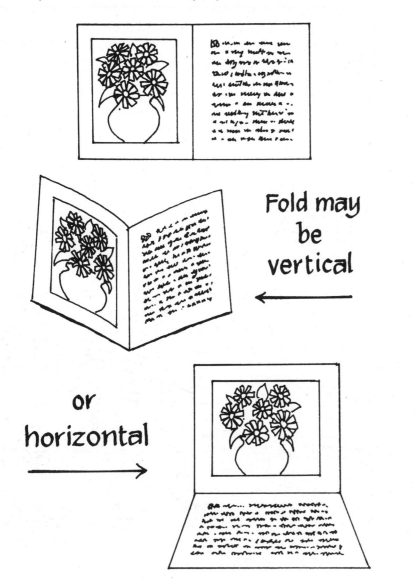

Fold may
be
vertical

or
horizontal

You can give 2-D work a 3-D look by placing a small box or cylinder behind the piece of work.

box
or
cylinder

art
work

backing sheet

The work itself can be formed into a cylindrical shape and fixed to the wall with staples.

Staple

Staple

The use of brackets to suspend work from the display-board or wall is another effective technique, especially with topics like weather, birds or insects.

By scoring and bending, large cut-out pictures produced as topic work or creative writing can be displayed to give a 3-D effect.

Start with the background and cut out the various component parts of the display – pirate, galleon, treasure chest, palm tree, grass – from separate sheets.

The use of collage on the pirate and treasure chest and fringing of the palm tree will further add to the 3-D effect.

You can display 2-D work which has been double or single mounted in large folders or books. Fold six large sheets of activity paper down the middle and staple them together down the central fold.

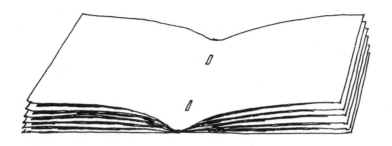

The book may then be hung at the side of a main display after the mounted work has been inserted and the cover decorated.

Mobiles and suspended displays

There is no limit to the topics which lend themselves to making mobiles, either 2-D or 3-D. Certain lightweight objects, such as paper straw constructions or cog wheel cut-outs, can make interesting mobiles. Multi-level mobiles suspended from a single line are the most difficult as they need to be very well balanced.

You will need florist's wire and cotton. The first step is to get the first bar balanced. Then suspend the bar from the ceiling or another suitable place and attach further bars, one at a time. Tie the cotton loosely so that it may be moved along the bars to achieve balance. Once balance has been achieved, tie the cotton tightly.

Alternatively, straw constructions may be suspended from a strong thread stretched across the ceiling.

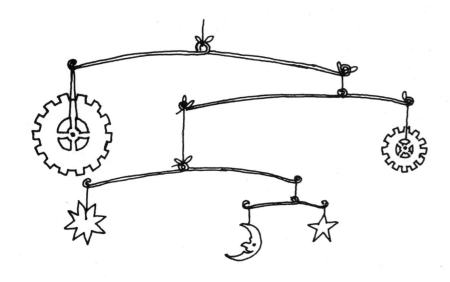

If the ceiling is too high, a strong thread taken from one side of the room to the other will support them. One end of the crêpe paper can be looped over the thread and stapled to the other end.

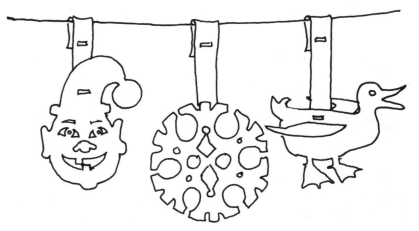

Information or words can also be displayed in this way provided it is boldly written (preferably in black) and can be easily read.

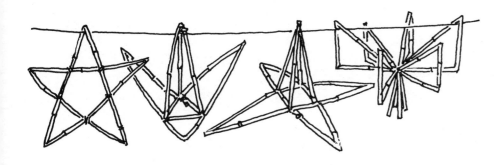

Artwork, double or single mounted, may be suspended by crêpe paper strips. Match the colour of the crêpe paper to the mounting for a very attractive effect. Cut 3 to 8 cm strips of crêpe paper of uniform or varying lengths, and staple them to the artwork at one end and to the ceiling at the other. By varying the length of the strips of crêpe paper a pleasing effect can be achieved.

15

Give extra dimension to 2-D mobiles by placing two figures back to back and filling the space between them with crumpled paper. Glue or staple the shapes together. You can then suspend them from the ceiling.

Displaying 3-D objects

When displaying 3-D natural objects, manufactured objects or children's work, they should be placed on horizontal surfaces which are at a suitable height in relation to the children's eye-level.

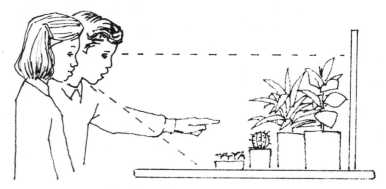

The base can be the top of a cupboard or two tables taped together, with a strip of corrugated cardboard wrapped round to conceal the base, the surface covered with sugar paper and the edge disguised with a frill of crêpe paper. Interesting objects may be displayed on contrasting circles made of card or activity paper. Drapes, dried grasses and plants can greatly enhance displays.

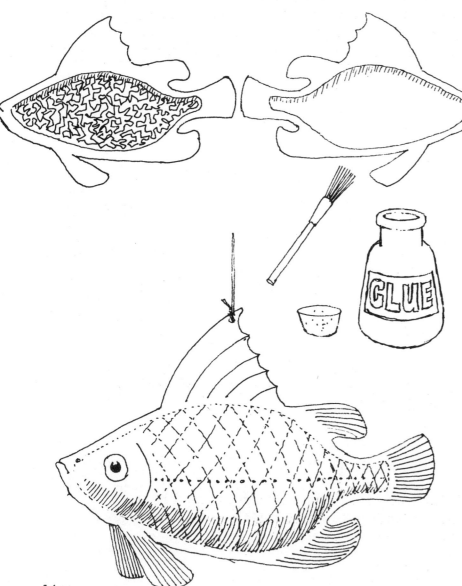

To display objects at different levels, roll up pieces of corrugated card and use them as plinths.

Plinths

Sturdy plinths can be made by using empty baby-milk cans. Simply stick the cans together in twos and threes using clear tape. Leave some single ones and use large and small cans to make plinths with different diameters.

To decorate the plinths, cover them with black corrugated card and fix the join with latex adhesive. Cut circles of black card slightly larger than the tops and fix them on with sticky tape, so that you can quickly remove them as they fade, or in case you want to use a different colour for the tops in a particular display. To give extra stability, half-fill the bottom tin with sand before you start. Keep each plinth as a separate unit so that you can arrange them to suit each display. These items will last a long time if they are treated carefully and their tops are changed regularly.

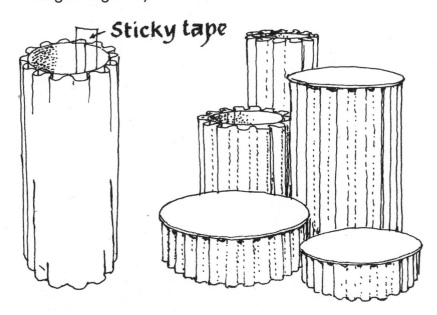

Sticky tape

Dioramas

A diorama is simply a scene in a cardboard box. They are easily moved and information can be displayed on the outside of the box if required.

Choose a box of suitable size for the subject and materials available. Boxes with white insides provide the best surfaces for painting. A top is not necessary unless you are creating an indoor scene or you need to suspend objects from it.

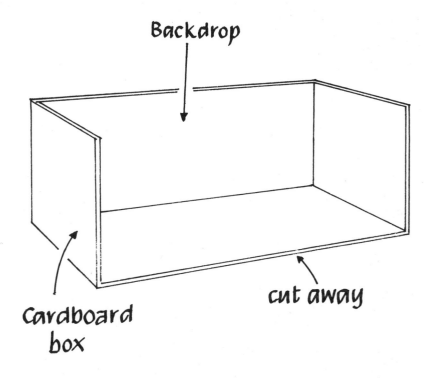

Backdrop

Cardboard box

cut away

Cut away one of the long sides of the box so that the main backdrop can be painted on the other long side. Paint the outside of the box before starting on the scene inside.

The subjects for dioramas are endless and with a little imagination they can make a really good focus for topic work. A possible idea for a diorama might be bonfire night.

Alternatively, different-sized boxes may be positioned beneath drapes and a diorama created on this 'landscape'. This can also be used as a base to display 3-D objects.

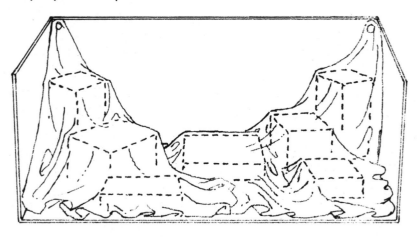

Fixing work to walls and surfaces

Before fixing the work to the wall it is a good idea to place it on the floor in front of the display space and move it around until the desired effect is achieved. Take care to avoid cramming too much work into a limited space. Try to place the work so that the areas in between are used to draw attention to the work. Also try to avoid diagonal lines and placing things on a slanted angle wherever possible. The arrangement should be planned by working inwards from both sides.

Next you need to decide on an appropriate method for fixing the work to the wall or display-board. With display-boards, the most usual and the neatest way is to use a staple gun. The only drawbacks are the holes left when staples are extracted and the difficulty of extracting them from harder surfaces.

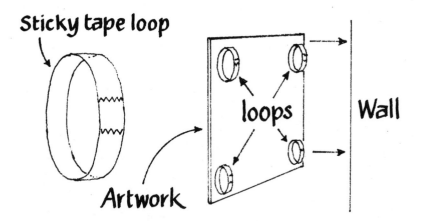

Sticky tape loop

Artwork

loops

Wall

Drawing-pins are not really suitable to use as the shiny surface and the size detract from the work being displayed.

When you do not want holes in a surface double-sided tape or sticky tape could be used. Form the sticky tape into a circle and stick one side on to the back of the work.

Spray glue is another product which can be used to stick lightweight work to various surfaces. A latex adhesive can be used to stick work to most slippery surfaces such as windows. Only a small amount is required and care should be taken to ensure that the window is free from condensation when the work is placed in position. The adhesive will peel off quite easily when you dismantle the display.

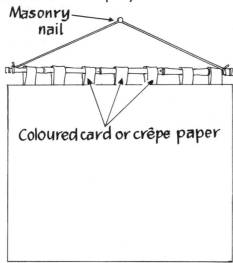

Masonry nail

Coloured card or crêpe paper

In many schools there are large areas of brick wall on which it is very difficult to display work. Latex adhesive can be used on painted surfaces, but for untreated brick walls, mount the work on card and hang the card on a bamboo cane or pole.

Fixing heavy things to walls
Large composite display items like mosaics or wooden collages need to be fixed with screws and wall-plugs if they are to be a permanent feature. Smaller items, such as tiles, can be fixed to chipboard using small nails. If the tiles are made of self-hardening clay make the holes before hardening.

Labelling and lettering
The labelling for any display should be clear and concise; the form of lettering used will largely depend on the nature of the display. It can be used to instruct, warn, advise, control, inform, direct, identify, persuade, announce, decorate, remind, advertise, commemorate and command.

The title of the display should be in large bold block letters to announce what the display is all about.

Large wooden templates are available in both capital and lower-case letters. These are invaluable for making signs and headings easily and quickly. See pages 107 to 116 for large letters which can be photocopied and cut out.

There are many different styles of writing and lettering ranging from roman capitals through gothic script to the computer style of the twentieth century.

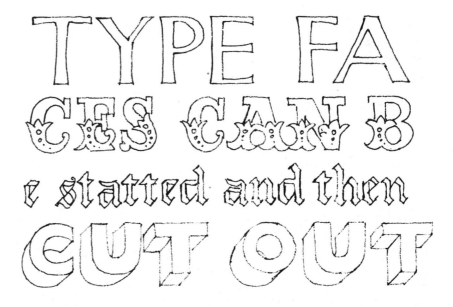

TYPE FA CES CAN B e statted and then CUT OUT

Whichever style you use, the spacing and setting out of the letters is very important so that they can be read easily and understood.

When letters have straight sides it is quite easy to space the letters evenly, but if a letter is not straight-sided and equal space is left in between, then the letter seems to be isolated because there is too much space around it.

HAND

The space around the 'A' can be reduced by bringing the two letters on either side a litttle closer, so that the letters now appear more equally spaced.

HAND

When writing labels free-hand, it is helpful to mark the paper very lightly with guidelines so that you can see where the capital letters begin and end, and a horizontal line drawn in between these will help to keep the lower-case letters all the same size.

The simple rule for spacing words is to leave enough space for the letter 'O'.

The Sun is

Plastic stencils are also available and these can be used by the children for writing titles on folders or topic books.

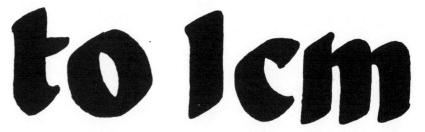

Bold use of thick marker pens can be very effective and they come in a range of thicknesses from fine **to 1cm**

Adhesive lettering can be used for a really professional finish, although it is expensive.

There is no limit to the variety of styles and designs which can be adapted. Here are some examples, but remember that a suitable style is important for the message or information you wish to convey. However well the lettering has been done, the wrong style of lettering can make it look ridiculous. For example, a display on space travel would look strange accompanied by gothic lettering.

For younger children it is best to do all lettering on labels in the style of the reading scheme they are using, which is usually rounded script.

Older children can be introduced to the different styles and taught to use some of them as a draughtsmanship lesson. See photocopiable pages 117 to 122 for examples of different lettering.

Displaying vocabulary for topics
Vocabulary is very often needed in display work to help the children with topic work. To add more visual appeal why not write it in a topic-related shape?

Using large sheets of white art paper, draw the shape in pencil first and then go over it with a large black felt-tipped pen.

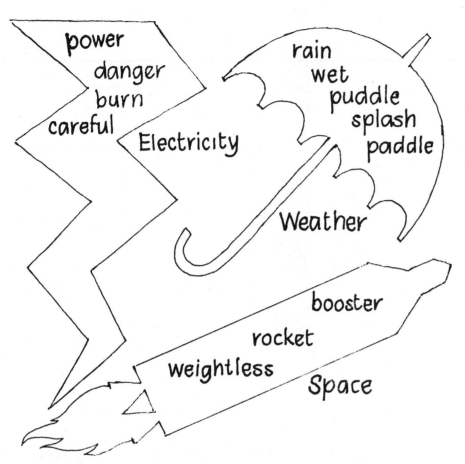

power
danger
burn
careful
Electricity

rain
wet
puddle
splash
paddle
Weather

booster
rocket
weightless
Space

Always write the words in dark colours so that they can be read across the room. Hold a class discussion to compile the original selection of words, but then add one or two new ones each night. Ask the children to spot them each morning, adding the stimulus of a game to extending vocabulary. For example, on a bonfire picture, the words could be written in between the flames, both of which could be in fire colours. This makes the picture more of a game than an aid to story-writing, but a more easily read shape could be used for this purpose.

Exhibition or project boxes

Age range
Nine plus.

What you need
Black card, scissors, ruler, stapler.

What to do
Mark and cut out the shape as shown from the black card. Score along all the dotted lines.

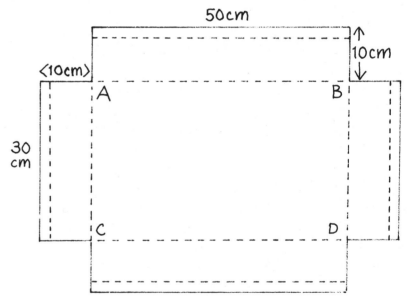

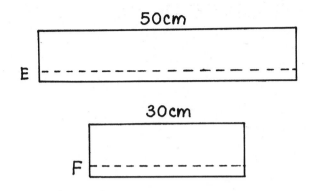

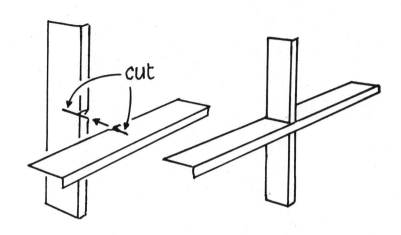

cut

Fold lines AB, BD, CD and AC. Fold inward and score along each of the edges, then fold the edges inward.

Assemble the box and insert the shelves. Strengthen the joins with a small stapler.

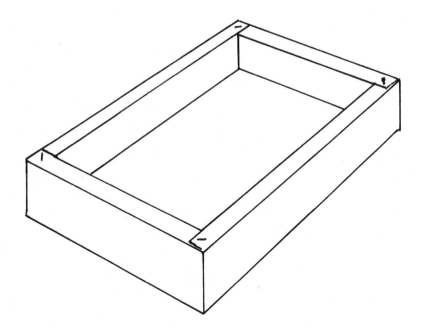

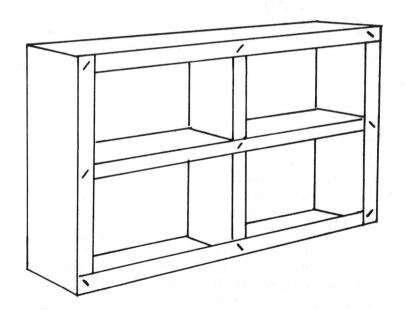

Fit the two shelves together in the form of a cross by making a cut in the shorter one.

Create a 'nook'

Age range
Nine plus.

What you need
Paper, scissors, stapler.

What to do
Using paper, cut roughly double the length required. Cut the height and shape required.

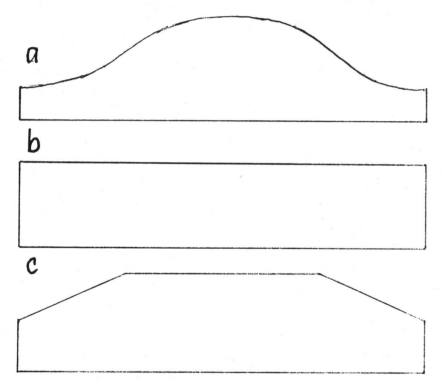

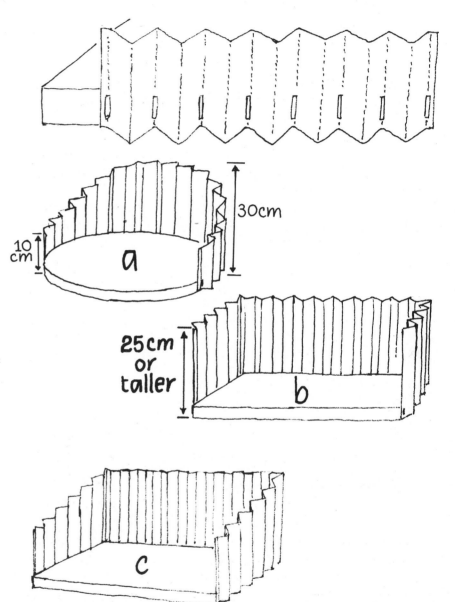

Pleat the paper neatly. Fix by stapling into the crease touching the table. Leave pleats standing proud.

Create display space

Age range
Nine plus.

What you need
Corrugated card, large cardboard boxes, stapler.

What to do
Use corrugated card in a variety of ways. It should be anchored with staples to give stability and retain the form.

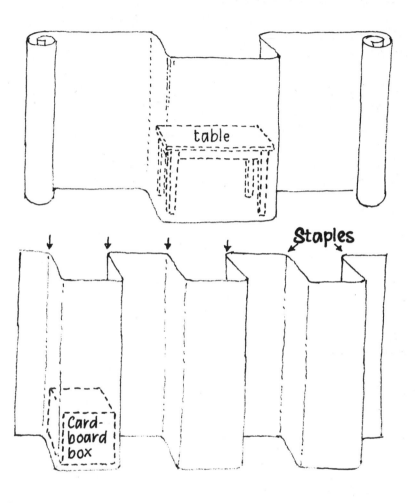

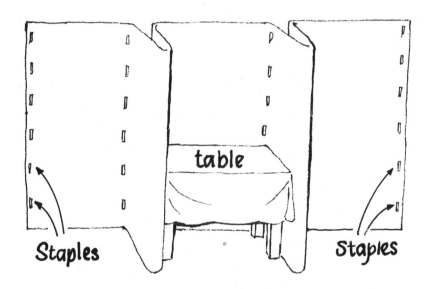

Buttresses can extend and break up a large flat wall area. A table or chair placed behind can form the buttress if the wall is unsuitable for staples.

Plain walls can be given interesting curves by bending corrugated card in.

If there is a shortage of space, card folded into a concertina shape will allow two or three times the usual amount of work to be squeezed into a limited area.

Large cardboard boxes can be covered with paper or material to make a versatile display area for 3-D work.

Displays around school

One part of the teacher's job is to make economic and imaginative use of space, providing practical work areas, storage areas, quiet corners and display space, often in close proximity. It is a difficult job in any type of building, so here are a few ideas to help you.

Entrance hall

The entrance hall is generally the first place visitors meet and if it is well cared for and attractively decorated, it generates a sense of well-being and gives some idea of the character of the school. Shapes and sizes vary considerably and use depends on many factors. Sometimes it is a thoroughfare for staff and pupils, an extra library area or a quiet waiting place for visitors. Whatever its use, a few well set out exhibits will provide a point of interest. The display may be made by the teacher to give pupils an example of adult craft, or the children themselves can play a major role. Your choice of subject will vary according to season and occasion.

natural light source

front door

The entrance hall is often the school news-desk where you need to display information on the school holiday or a parents' meeting. However, it is a good idea to have exhibitions of children's work from each age group in school to show the range of abilities. They are always of great interest to parents. It is sometimes possible to borrow museum exhibits (stuffed animals, local artefacts, historical models) for use in schools, and you may well be able to obtain permission for children to handle the exhibits. Your LEA may have a collection of prints which could be borrowed by the school, or you could ask a local artist or craftsman to loan work for a short period.

Flowers or plants placed at strategic points can arrest the eye, and healthy foliage creates the impression of a caring, ordered environment. Any furniture should be carefully placed in relation to architectural features, such as your display-board or platforms and doors, windows and alcoves. A single display-board or corner carefully planned and lit can have dramatic impact.

If the entrance hall is dark then try to introduce a bright colour or an artificial light source. If notice-boards are necessary they should be of simple design and painted in a colour that tones with the general colour scheme. All notices should be clearly lettered and arranged on paper of a colour that also tones with the scheme.

Crêpe paper

Welcome to our School

card

There is a danger of becoming too stylised or fussy in displays, when one or two objects often convey a dramatic message by their simplicity. A large object can be exciting because of its intrusion, and boldness is often the essence of a good display.

Corridors

In many schools, corridors are main communal display spots as well as work areas, storage places and busy thoroughfares. For these reasons they pose a difficult display problem because of space restrictions, people passing by, the accumulation of dust and rubbish and, not least, the dreaded 'wind-tunnel effect' which operates whenever any two doors are opened at once! It is best to keep displays fairly high and well secured, possibly combining 2-D and 3-D work on walls, and including mobiles. Long narrow corridors may not allow sufficient breadth of vision for friezes to be appreciated, so alternating wall items and mobiles will allow enjoyment of select pieces of work. If possible, include an end vista to take the focal point down the corridor. A long corridor can be shortened by using predominately warm colours and large shapes for the vista, while a short one can be lengthened by using colder distancing colours, like blues and greens, and smaller shapes.

If corridors are flanked by classroom windows, it can be useful to cover these with long runs of 2 m wide corrugated card to lessen the impact of classroom displays seen through windows and competing for attention with those in the corridor. It could also provide an extra surface for corridor display or an interlude of plain wall. Space can often heighten the dramatic impact of work which is displayed. Don't be too keen to merely fill every space available in a patchwork quilt effect because this doesn't encourage aesthetic awareness and thought about design.

In very narrow corridors it is usually practical to keep as much floor space clear as possible. But if you happen to have too much space or you wish to slow traffic for any reason, build out-crops with corrugated card, and create nooks and crannies for greater interest and display area.

Hide items stored in the corridor by putting them beneath tables edged with curtaining. It will look better if the colour tones with the general decorations, creating a harmony of colour and line. Curtaining can be hung on a wire or stapled under or on the edge of the table-top.

Pleat curtain & staple

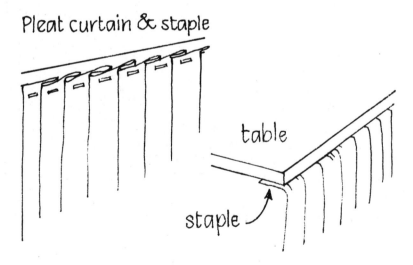

table

staple

Assembly halls

An assembly hall is seen regularly by all members of the school, and in many buildings joins the entrance hall and is on show from there, too. It has its advantages in providing space and scope for large dramatic displays and exciting visual experiences. It also enjoys a captive audience in assemblies. However, problems stem from this size too. Small exhibits are lost and space is often shared with PE equipment, furniture and other uses such as school dinners and extramural activities. You need to be adventurous and make bold use of colour, height and size. Often a single giant focal point is all that is needed, if possible using the ceiling and wall faced by the school during assemblies. If this is also the wall facing the main entrance then all the better for impact. If a stage platform or moveable stage blocks are available then these can be incorporated in the display to add height and importance.

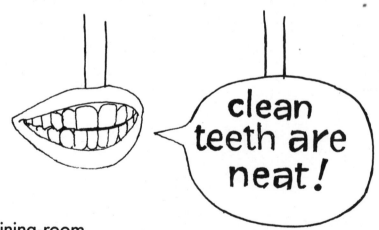

Dining-room

If your school has a separate dining-room it is usually another large space with potential as a display area. Main display items need to be away from the action, such as on the top half of walls, round windows or as mobiles.

Windows

If you wish to add a little privacy to your classroom or block out an unsightly view, then why not paint your windows? Colours remain strong for many months and the only damage will be done by excessive condensation. Stained-glass windows made with black paper, tissue or clear wrapping can be very attractive too, but for quick, lasting results painting on glass is a new aesthetic experience which can be done by adults or pupils.

In the latter case it is a good idea to keep them high or round the sides as dinner staff won't be impressed by having to lift chairs through a web of crêpe paper and glitter. As in the main hall, impact must be made with bold displays. Topics in here could include: foods for health, seasonal food, growing our food, or hygiene.

For display ideas, interest can be added on walls by using corrugated cardboard shaped display-boards. Use bold, bright colours for painting and backing sheets as dining-rooms are usually well lit and colours will fade quickly.

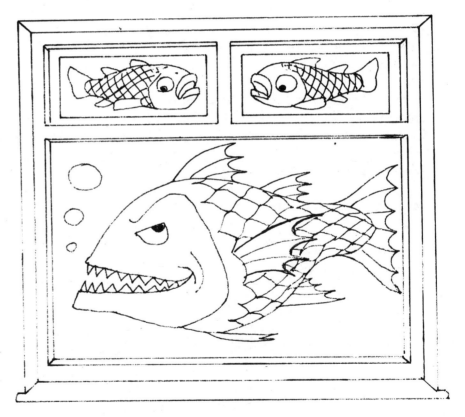

Libraries

The library needs to provide several things: comfortable seating, possibly a table for librarians, some management notices ('quiet please', 'infant library', 'returned books', etc), some display items to encourage reading and, last but not least, the books arranged in an orderly and attractive manner.

Although classical shelving is very practical, some books can remain hidden in a large collection. Similarly, shelving which is too high for smaller children to reach is quite useless for book storage. If your school has high shelving, use the top two or three shelves for display. Use the highest for the library notices and lower ones for showing off books. If you include a few plants and change books about once a week you will have an easily managed point of interest. It will focus children's attention and keep books circulating.

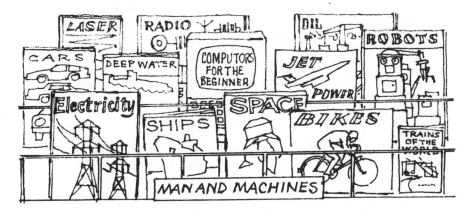

If you have a small display-board or the room to put one up made from corrugated card, turn it into a book review spot. Put on display those books reviewed and include some cut-out paintings or drawings of the characters, with the characters' names, the book title and the author. This display should be at eye-level for readability, and 3-D decorations will add appeal.

If you have room, a topic research display could be introduced. Keep other display to a minimum to focus attention on this.

If you have the space, a wire book-rack can be of use as it displays books face on and it is the front cover which sells a book to most children, particularly younger ones and poorer readers. You can use it to display your collection of books on a topic. Strategically placed book marks are also a good idea (see photocopiable page 124).

Nooks, crannies and odd corners

We can all find odd corners which would be handy for displaying a single interesting item or a special piece of work. You may have just three or four pieces of 3-D work you want to admire, so here are some ideas.

Table and cupboard tops

Keep the display very simple. For surface cover use cork tiles, rush matting, corrugated card or coloured art paper (cover the edges of the table or tape the edges to prevent curling and tearing). Put 2-D items flat to give a new perspective. Remember to use cupboard doors too.

Unusual surfaces

Use unusual surfaces like the piano top (if it is against a wall) or a corner on the floor. Make corrugated card display-boards on a small scale.

Make an area look bigger or more imposing

Extend some parts of the picture over the edges to create a 3-D effect. In this case it is the rainbow which extends, but it could be tree branches, roots or flowers, clouds, exhaust trails from planes or rockets, sunbeams etc.

Screened areas

You may need an area partitioned but still need light and a feeling of space, so something like this tree provides both. Leaves can be changed seasonally and the partition then becomes a permanent nature display spot, especially if you add plants and animals to the bottom area.

Window-sills

Window-sills can make an ideal nook for display. Decide how attractive your view is and either incorporate it or block it out.

Equipment stores

Obviously you will want equipment stored for easy access, but if you think of this in terms of your general display policy, you will be able to add a dimension of classification as well.

Store items in boxes or plastic containers, such as washing-up bowls and stacker boxes. Buy the same colour combinations to help children to identify 'homes' for equipment and to give an overall harmony to an area of school which can sometimes look jumbled. If you can store under tables, cover the fronts with a toning cloth or curtains. You can further enclose an area with a corrugated cardboard screen. Use the main colour you have chosen for the card and marker pen for the labels. Apart from looking neat and clear, simple labels are also highly functional.

The backs of cupboard doors (lockable!) are handy for the display and storage of small articles. This neat display is highly functional as it shows at a glance which keys are missing.

Garden nooks

School gardens make good display areas. Create little nooks in odd corners by introducing new height, texture and shape. The parks department may be really useful here as they sometimes have odd containers, broken paving stones and, at times, one or two shrubs.

Local industry may prove to be a source for large, plastic chemical containers (non-toxic contents), sawn in half to make excellent tubs. Ask parents to help. This garden addition needn't cost much at all, and the entrance to the school can be made more welcoming in this way. Vary the height and contents of containers, adding some evergreen items if you can.

It may be possible to remove selected paving stones and replace them with coloured pebbles or rocks, collected on field trips or holidays, to provide a textural variation. You could plan a small-scale mosaic in pebbles. The key in a paving project is to provide a variety of texture. Try to keep to natural colours to give an interesting but harmonising background for plants.

Displays for topic work

Contrasts

Age range
Six plus.

Group size
Artwork in pairs,
teacher to do display.

What you need
Black and white powder paint, mixing palette, black and
white art paper, black crêpe paper, stapler.

What to do
Provide an assortment of brush sizes and teach the
children how to mix paint into shades, from palest grey to
almost black. Allow plenty of practice on rough paper to
check the effect of mixing, then let them have two or three
goes at brushing from one side of the paper to the other
with lines of pai   Encourage them to change the
thickness of the line, its shape and the shade of grey.

Single mount the work on white paper for the wall and
on black for the mobiles. Hang these in a staggered
arrangement from the ceiling, using black crêpe paper. If
possible mount white paper on the wall behind the
mobiles to continue the contrast theme.

A peacock

What you need
Green or white backing paper for the wall, two shades of blue and yellow for the peacock body, white art paper, wax crayons, thick black felt-tipped pen, stapler, A4 paper.

What to do
Get each child to do a growth pattern. Start with a crayon dot at the bottom of the page, then start the next and each following line from that dot. The idea is to fill the whole page by making the pattern grow a little more each time. Each line should be a different colour, shape, thickness and texture from the preceding one. Encourage the children to make bold use of colour and to press quite hard. Display as shown using two semicircles of blue backing paper and a cut-out body. Draw the head feathers and feet using a thick black felt-tipped pen. Staple the patterns up to display them.

Colour table

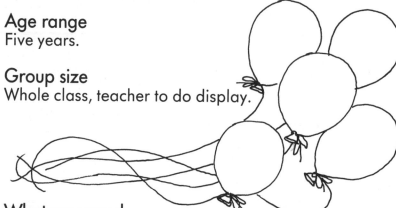

What you need
Five blue balloons, a blue vase, blue art paper, crêpe paper, foil, stapler, latex adhesive, sticky tape.

What to do
Make a circle of foil by joining together two sheets with the latex adhesive and place this sheet on the table. Press it over the edge and trim it leaving a 5 cm overhang. Trim it to a zig-zag shape. Make a crêpe paper frill about 25 cm deep or half the length of the roll. Staple the frill to the table at about 15 cm intervals, joining crêpe paper by overlapping at the short point on the frill. Put a blob of adhesive under the edge of the foil and fold it over the edge on to the crêpe paper.

Make five tight rolls of blue art paper of varying lengths up to a metre. Fold over the top and fix the balloons with sticky tape as shown.

Stick some foil to a piece of card and cut out letters using the stencils given on pages 107-116. Put the letters down an even distance apart and, using clear nylon thread, fix them together. Join a long length of thread to the top of each letter and fix them separately to the ceiling or join the threads to a piece of card which can then be stapled to the ceiling.

Arrange your selection of blue items on circles of art paper.

blue

Wool

Blue
art paper

Blue foil

Blue
crêpe paper

Blue

Colours

Age range
Five to six years.

Group size
Teacher to assemble, children to do collage work and paint boxes.

What you need
Three very large cardboard boxes, red, blue and yellow powder paint, large brushes and sponges, red, blue, yellow and white art paper, red, blue and yellow collage material, adhesive, stapler, sticky tape, four stage blocks.

What to do
Paint the large boxes in each of the primary colours. If you have stage blocks cover one all over with red, one with yellow, and two with blue paper. If you haven't, use cardboard boxes instead. Draw a figure or animal for each colour and make a collage. Mount one on the front of each of the painted boxes. Place the blue stage blocks in the centre with the red and yellow ones on either side in front of a screen or wall. Then place the painted boxes on top of the stage blocks matching the colours. Cut out the words 'red', 'blue', and 'yellow' from red, blue and yellow art paper and fix in curves with stick tape on the wall above each box.

Spring

Age range
Any age.

Group size
Teacher to do display.

What you need
Corrugated card, white and green art paper, paints and pastels, sponges, sticky tape, latex adhesive, brown, green and pink tissue-paper, container of sand, two water containers, bare twigs, a bunch of daffodils, two primula plants, stuffed birds and animals or Plasticine, an old bird's nest.

What to do
Cover a small table or cupboard top with green art paper, using sticky tape to fix it in position. Make a corrugated card nook as shown. Cut an oval of white art paper almost to fill the back. Paint a rough spring landscape, using sponges to give a misty effect. Mix a very pale blue for the sky and dab with sponge very lightly to get the effect of clouds, then mix three shades of green and dab in the hills. Use pastels to draw in the rainbow and the stream. Fix the picture lightly to the corrugated card with latex adhesive. Older children can paint the picture themselves.

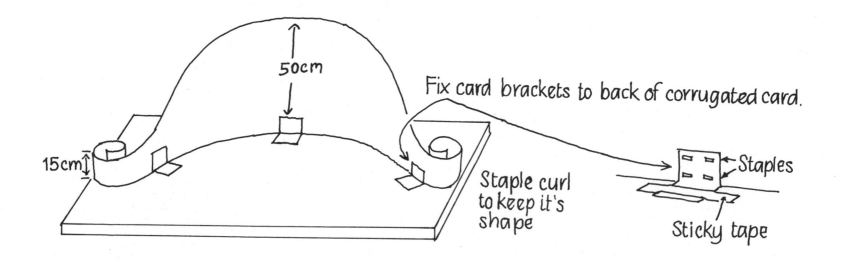

50cm

15cm

Fix card brackets to back of corrugated card.

Staple curl to keep it's shape

Staples

Sticky tape

Stick pink tissue-paper flowers to the bare branches and stand them in a container of sand. Cover the container with crumpled brown and green tissue-paper. Put the daffodils in a container of water, covered in the same way. Place a primula plant at either side and cover the pots.

Borrow some stuffed exhibits from your local museum if possible. If not, make pottery or Plasticine models or get the children to draw large pictures with pastels, cut these out and stick them on card. These can then be stuck with latex adhesive to something heavy like a wooden building brick, to support them upright.

The sun

Age range
Six plus.

Group size
Variable.

What you need
Sunflowers – dried, fresh or made by the children, orange and yellow activity paper, clear plastic film, card, paper, a range of paints, a collection of things which protect us from the sun such as a sun-hat, glasses, lotion etc, pictures of the solar system, seeds.

What to do
The first part of the display could contain a large vase with the sunflowers arranged in it. Poems and writing about the sun could be displayed, mounted on sun shapes cut from orange and yellow activity paper. You could add a backing sheet of yellow with a flame coloured drape to set the right colour tones.

The children could make simple sun dials which might be displayed alongside actual examples. The other aspects which might be included are the objects used to protect or cool us in hot sun eg sunglasses, sun-hats, fans, etc. Children can make their own sun visors with card and clear plastic film.

Pictures and posters of the solar system may be displayed alongside or around a large illustration or collage of one of the stories or legends of the sun.

A final part of the display could include stories and paintings or posters of the enjoyable things we can do in the sun: going for picnics, swimming, sunbathing, summer holidays, boating, camping etc.

Contrast this with what happens when there is too much sun: drought, famine, forest fires, desert, sunburn, heatstroke.

Older children could look at solar power and perhaps try to design a machine powered by the sun. The 2-D display could include drawings of the machine and the children could then try to make the machine for the 3-D display.

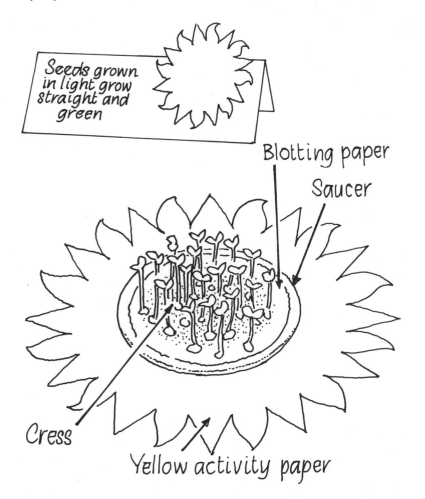

Plants require light to grow, so a simple experiment could be set up to show this. Use a display to highlight the results.

Seaside panorama

Age range
Six plus.

Group size
Whole class involved, individuals to draw kites and beach balls, two at a time to paint background and stick pictures on, a teacher or an adult to do title, stick on lighthouse, make Punch and Judy stand and hang mobiles.

What you need
Blue crêpe paper, kite tails, powder paints, wax crayons, pencil crayons, felt-tipped pens, latex adhesive, stapler, staple-gun, sponges, brown and green tissue-paper, white art paper, see-through plastic container, corrugated card, foil, crêpe paper, wool.

What to do

Mount a piece of white paper and draw a huge sun in wax crayon. Draw on the horizon, a cliff and beach lines. Using sponges do a light wash for the sky. You may want to do this yourself or to allow two children to do it, standing on a table with an adult in attendance. Sponge dabs in white make effective clouds. Use blues, greens and white for the sea and use sponge to make waves. Rub patches of the beach section with yellow wax crayon (as long as the wall behind isn't brick!) and then wash with a pale yellow. Paint the cliffs green on top and white in front using a brush.

Paint a piece of paper in red and white stripes, and staple it in a roll to make the lighthouse. Stick the top into position. When this is dry stick it to the paper backing. Spread adhesive where you want rocks to be, then lightly crumple some brown tissue-paper and touch it into place leaving it puffed up. Hide the base of the cylinder with 'rocks'. If you have any very light shells these can be glued on to the rocks. Paint a lot of sea spray near the rocks.

After a class discussion children can draw their own items and figures to add. Try to encourage a good spread of land, sea and air items and point out the need for smaller figures at a distance, larger in the foreground etc. Children can cut out and stick on their own figures, and you can add speech bubbles with children's own words to make it a 'talking picture'.

Cut the title sheet out already waved or as a straight piece to be stapled in a wave later. Cut out kite shapes for the younger children but older ones can be taught to draw their own. Divide these into quadrants and use crayons, pastels, felt-tipped pens or paint to make a different pattern in each quadrant. Cut lengths of wool ready and let children staple their own tails and lines. To hang the kites, staple them to the ceiling and wall.

Younger children can draw a circle divided into sections for the beach balls. Paint each section in a different colour. Hang them from the ceiling with crêpe paper.

Construct a Punch and Judy stand from corrugated card as shown and decorate it with foil stripes and crêpe paper frills. Add crêpe paper curtains and a sign.

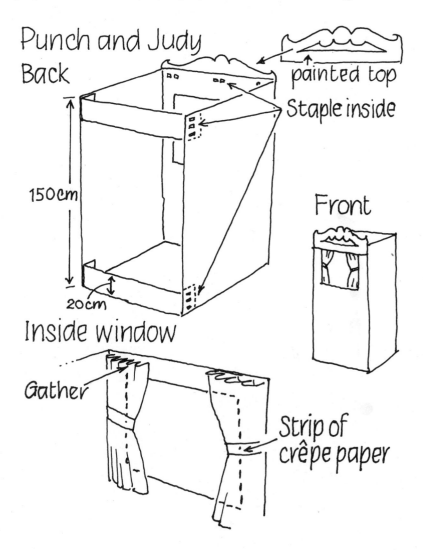

Punch and Judy
Back

painted top

Staple inside

150cm

20cm

Front

Inside window

Gather

Strip of crêpe paper

Water

Age range
Six plus.

Group size
Small groups or whole class.

What you need
Pictures and posters of the different moods of water (calm and tranquil ponds and lakes, rough stormy seas or cascading water falls), posters of the uses of water (ie for cleaning or putting out fires), water sports, children's pictures and writing, beans or peas, jam-jars, blotting paper, some simple experiments with water, collection of objects used in water, plastic sheeting.

What to do
The teacher might draw a simple illustration to show the hydrological cycle

This can be surrounded by pictures of the uses of water, drawn by the children. Ask the children to write about the way water comes to our houses today and how it was collected long ago. A display of wax-resistant paintings can be included as a way of showing how things can be made waterproof, and the children can experiment by painting wet on wet paper to see what results can be achieved. Water makes things grow so a corner could be set up with a growing chart and beans or peas placed in a jam-jar with blotting paper. The growth of these can be plotted on a chart.

A display of objects used in water for having fun can range from a rubber duck used for play in the bath to a life jacket used for sailing and even, where space will allow, an inflatable dingy or a lilo. Again children's drawings and writing can be displayed, along with posters and photographs.

① Sun shines on the water

② Water evaporates

③ Warm air rises

④ As it rises it cools – clouds form

⑤ Rain falls the water runs into streams

⑥ Streams join to make a river

⑦ River flows back into the sea

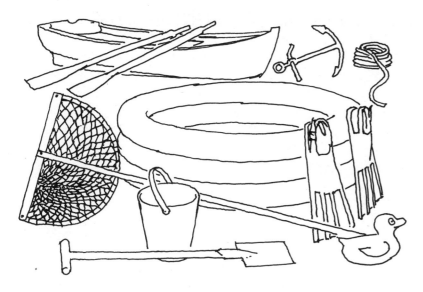

A table of simple water experiments will add to the display and allow the children to become involved even more. The surface of the display table or cupboard should be covered with plastic sheeting so that if water is spilled accidentally, it can be mopped up without too much damage.

Floating or sinking
A box of objects, all mixed up, could be placed by a large tank or aquarium. The children can then test which things float or sink, and sort and classify them accordingly.

Water has a skin
Fill a plastic beaker almost to the top and then start to add water a few drops at a time using a dropper (figure 1). As the beaker fills, the surface of the water will rise higher than the rim of the beaker. The children can observe that it looks as if the water has a skin, and this is what prevents it from dripping down the sides (figure 2).

Refraction
Take a shallow clear plastic bowl and half fill it with water. Place a ruler in the bowl of water and it will appear that the ruler is bent.

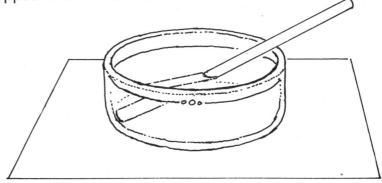

Children's writing
Include writing or poems about rain or the sea. A display about rain might include a picture of a child in wellingtons and a raincoat with an umbrella, and the children's writing alongside with rainbows and cloud shapes stuck around as a border.

Rain mobiles

Age range
Five to seven.

What you need
Cartridge paper, crêpe paper, paint, PVA adhesive or clear wood varnish, activity paper, stapler.

What to do
Umbrellas
Cut two umbrella shapes for the children and get them to paint both shapes in the same colour. A pattern may then be added. Staple the front and back together including a couple of little pleats on the top edge. Stick the handle to the inside top edge and let it hang free. Hang the umbrellas as mobiles using coloured crêpe paper in sets for size or colour.

Wellies
Cut out the shapes for the children and get each child to paint both sides of each of his pair of wellies in the same colour. When they are dry, paint them with a thickish PVA adhesive/water mix on both sides which will dry to a sheen. For a high gloss use clear wood varnish. Allow the children to help with folding the legs. Use pink activity paper for bare legs or let the children decide on a colour if they are wearing tights or trousers. Hang them from the ceiling in pairs.

Rivers and streams

Age range
Seven plus.

Group size
Small groups or whole class.

What you need
Card, wire, paper, metallic paper or foil, adhesive, scissors, wax crayons, paints, glitter.

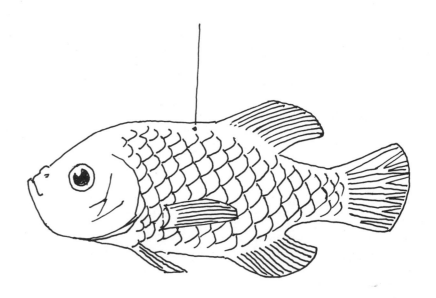

What to do
Look at the fish that live in rivers. Get the class to make 3-D versions of them, painted in realistic colours. Stuff the shapes as shown on page 16. Add glitter to suggest the gleam of fish scales.

Tessellated fish

Age range
Seven plus.

Group size
Small groups or individuals.

What you need
Card, pencil, ruler, adhesive, scissors, paints, felt-tipped pens, wax crayons, metallic felt-tipped pens, glitter.

What to do
Make the master template by drawing a rectangle on a piece of card and cut it out (for template see photocopiable page 123). Cut out a section from A to B (see figure 1).

Figure 1
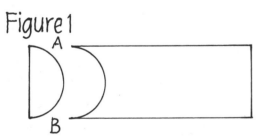

Move this to the opposite edge and stick it in place (figure 2).

Figure 2
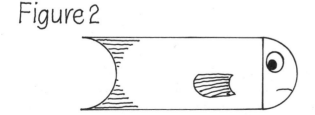

Each child could make a single fish and decorate it. Mount the class collection on to a backing sheet, or get each child to make up a sheet of nine fish (figure 3) and mount a group of these as schools of fish in a lake.

Figure 3
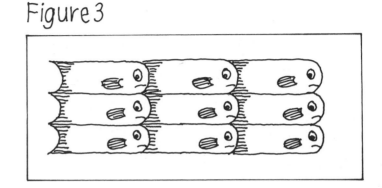

Other creatures live in rivers and streams and the children could find out about these.

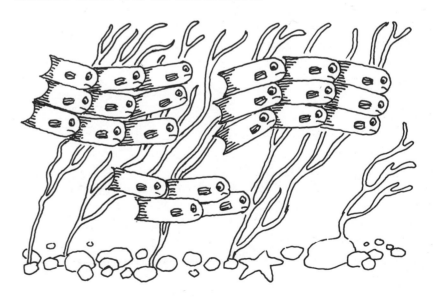

Building bridges

Age range
Five to seven.

Group size
Small groups or whole class.

What you need
Paper, Lego, Meccano, building blocks, pictures of bridges, ports etc.

What to do
The children could experiment with strips of paper to try to make a bridge. Get them to fold and score the paper to make it more rigid and able to support weight. They could experiment using building blocks, Lego, or Meccano. These bridges could then be displayed.

Children living near a port could visit the docks and paint pictures of the buildings, the cranes and the ships and make a large frieze.

Children could find out which items are brought in through that port and which are exported, and on a map of the world, show the routes of the boats.

Follow-up
Children could pretend to be exploring a strange jungle river with all kinds of exotic creatures and this could lead to creative writing or poetry. This could be displayed as a folder illustrated with children's paintings or drawings.

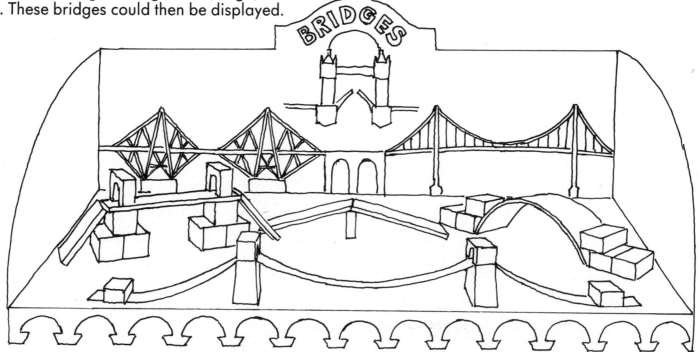

Autumn

Age range
Any age.

Group size
Small groups for artwork, teacher to do display.

What you need
Paints, card, paper, wax crayons, activity paper, leaves, crêpe paper, seeds, sticky-back plastic, branches.

What to do
You can begin an autumn display almost as soon as the children return from the summer break. A good starting point would be a walk around the school grounds to see if they can spot any changes showing that summer is coming to an end: flowers going to seed, the first hint of leaves changing colour etc. As the weeks pass the signs will become more noticeable.

The children should be encouraged to keep a careful note of these changes and also the dates on which they are first noticed.

Old calendars often have beautiful autumnal pictures for the months of September and October, which could

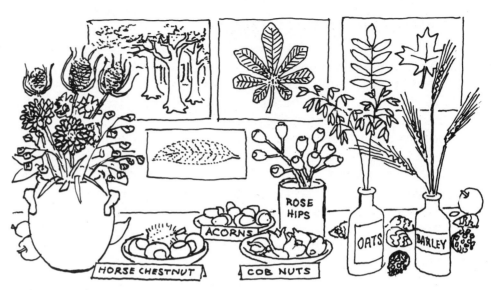

be used as a focal point for a collection of dried grasses and flowers, and branches, as shown.

Leaf rubbings and leaf prints using the warm autumn colours make a good display either against a dark brown background or as mobiles hanging from the ceiling.

With a little care these leaves can be positioned to make a pleasing arrangement.

To make a leaf rubbing position a leaf underneath a piece of paper with the veined side upwards. Use the wax crayon on its side and slowly draw across the surface of the paper applying pressure. The shape of the leaf will then be revealed as the wax colour is picked up where the veins are touching the paper. Again, careful positioning of the leaves can create some attractive effects. Encourage children to overlap leaves and choose the warm autumn colours of red, brown, yellow and orange.

When the leaves really start to fall, the children can make a simple hedgehog. Cut out a large hedgehog shape from activity paper and collect some dried leaves. Try to choose the flattest ones.

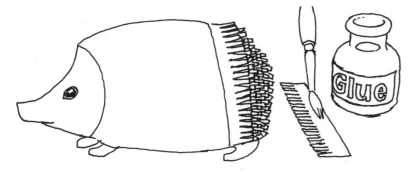

Start at the back of the hedgehog and stick down a line of leaves; overlap the next line working towards the front.

An arrangement of paper sculpture leaves, double mounted on a circle of activity paper can be hung as a mobile, using crêpe paper, or pinned to a display board.

Seed patterns can be made using sycamore 'keys' and acorns and berries. Arrange the pattern before sticking them down, one seed at a time. These can also be hung as mobiles.

NB Point out the dangers of berries being poisonous. Children should never eat them.

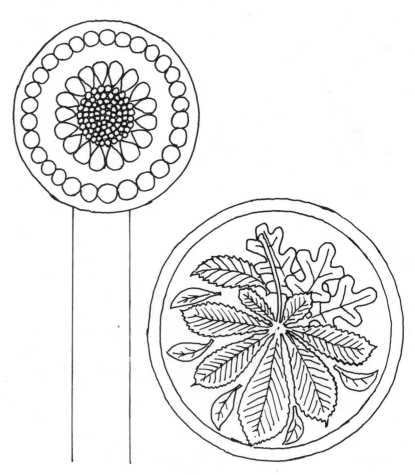

Seed and leaf patterns

Age range
Seven plus.

Group size
Individuals or small groups.

What you need
Textured wallpaper, activity paper, dried flowers, leaves and seeds, latex adhesive, scissors.

What to do
Using templates the children can cut out circles of wallpaper with 20 cm diameters and circles of activity paper with 23 cm diameters. Get them to place the dried flowers, leaves and seeds in a pleasing arrangement before sticking them down. They must use very small amounts of adhesive and lift up one item at a time, apply the adhesive, replace the item and then go on to the next. They will need to work very carefully. Display as shown, and point out the non-tessellation of circles.

Winter scene

Age range
Five plus.

Group size
Individuals for painting, older children to mount their own picture if the board is not too high.

What you need
White, blue and grey activity paper, paints, silver foil.

What to do
Decide on the content and format of the picture with the class and allocate individuals to paint different items. They can cut their own out if possible. Cut white paper for hill shapes, use blue paper for a night sky and then position the white hill shapes on top. Add some painted snow flakes and silver foil stars.

Assemble the picture as a class exercise, then the children can help to decide where things look best.

The Post Office

Age range
Six plus.

Group size
Small groups.

What you need
Posters available from the Post Office, pictures and posters of Postman Pat, stamps from around the world, map of the world, cartridge paper, adhesive, paints, scissors.

What to do
For very young children, use the popular TV character Postman Pat as a starting point, and initiate discussion on the pleasant things the postman brings – cards for Christmas and birthdays, presents in parcels, holiday postcards, etc.

Your display could be a large collage of pictures of Postman Pat and Jess the cat, children's paintings of Pat and items which bear the Postman Pat logo. A collection of the books could also be displayed alongside. The children's paintings could be mounted to look like large stamps, while older children can have fun designing their own stamps which can be hung as mobiles or mounted on a board to look like a page from a stamp album.

Posters available from the Post Office tell the story of the journey of a letter. Children's writing and illustrations can follow on from this. A display of the history of the mail would make a very interesting corner. Pictures and drawings of mail coaches, highwaymen and different types of pillar box could be included.

Older children could write letters to each other and devise their own postal systems for collection, sorting and distribution. Various corners of the classrooms could be allocated to this and displays in keeping with the theme could be mounted in these corners. Stamps from around the world could be mounted around a map of the world with strings or lines going from the stamp to the country of origin. Another idea is to look at the special commemorative stamps and build a display around them. Children could paint large versions of the stamps to be displayed alongside.

Come to the circus

Age range
Five years.

Group size
Small groups with teacher help.

What you need
Large sheets white paper, paint, collage materials, thick black marker pens, 2 m tubes from carpet or fabric rolls.

What to do
Draw outline circus characters using marker pens and get the children to collage or paint them. They should take an active part in the decisions about colour, texture etc.

Find an interesting surface for the display. The cut-out collage figures will also look interesting against plain brick walls. Stick painted card poles to the wall as shown with lots of sticky tape.

Space

Age range
Seven plus.

Group size
Small groups or whole class.

What you need
Card, paper, adhesive, metallic paper or silver foil, black activity paper, glitter.

What to do

Space flight is a very interesting topic for most children and it can be approached in several different ways. First of all you can take the factual point of view, such as the NASA space programme or that of the Soviet Union. It is possible to write to the NASA Space Centre for a fact pack which could form the nucleus of a display, supplemented once more by children's writing and drawing.

The children could also bring in toy spacemen, models of spacecraft, shuttles, buggies etc.

Another aspect of space is the universe and solar system – a study of the planets. A large display of the sun and the position of the planets which make up our solar system could lead to imaginative illustrations of the surface of the different planets and also pictures of possible inhabitants.

Older children especially will enjoy creating space creatures from the materials listed. An interesting CDT exercise is for the children to design a space vehicle and then try to construct the model from their own design.

The secret garden

Age range
Six plus.

Group size
Small groups or whole class.

What you need
Gardening catalogues,
adhesive,
scissors,
paints,
paper,
tissue-paper.

What to do
Draw and paint a doorway with the door ajar looking from the inside out. Cut out photos of flower heads from the gardening catalogues. If you prefer, tissue-paper flowers can be made and used instead of photos. These should be glued in the space of the open doorway to give the impression of looking out on to a beautiful garden. A pathway could be incorporated with a sundial at the end to give a feeling of perspective.

Poetry or writing can be displayed down each side of the large picture.

The faraway tree

Age range
Five plus.

Group size
Individuals for paintings,
groups of three for cutting out,
teacher to do display.

What you need
Pale blue backing paper, assortment of green paper,
black or brown paper, white art paper, crêpe paper,
powder paints, stapler.

What to do

Decide with the children on the format of the picture and the characters to involve. Allocate individuals to paint each one. There will probably only be room for two at a time in the art area, but this will depend on the organisation and help available.

Older children can be taught to cut out their own work. You may need to draw an outline for younger children to fill in. Get groups of children to cut out leaves, bushes and clouds.

Assembling the picture

Staple on the blue backing paper for the sky and a strip of green paper for the ground. Cut out the trunk and branches separately as shown and staple them together. Let the branches loop out to give a 3-D effect and curve the trunk before you fix it in position.

Fold the leaves down the middle and staple them to the branches. Fix the figures in the same way as the trunk to give them depth. Discuss what each character is going to say and write it in the speech bubbles.

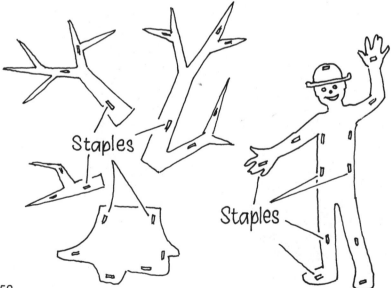

Pirates

Age range
Seven plus.

Group size
Small groups or the whole class.

What you need
Card, paper, paints, collage materials, adhesive, scissors.

What to do
Paint and make collages of a pirate captain and a treasure chest. The children can then draw posters of their pirate, 'Wanted, Dead or Alive'. A descriptive passage can accompany this and the posters may be displayed around the large picture.

A separate display could be made about the treasure island. The children could write adventure stories based upon their search for the lost treasure and their adventures using an ancient treasure map.

Display the stories round the large treasure map. Cut out the edges of the map to make it look old. Smudge the edges with brown pastel and curl them with a ruler. The stories could be displayed in book form.

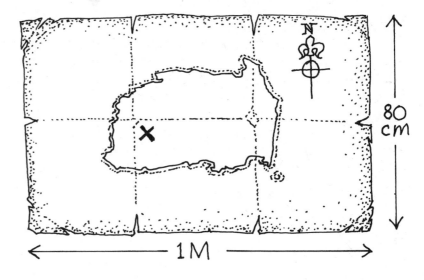

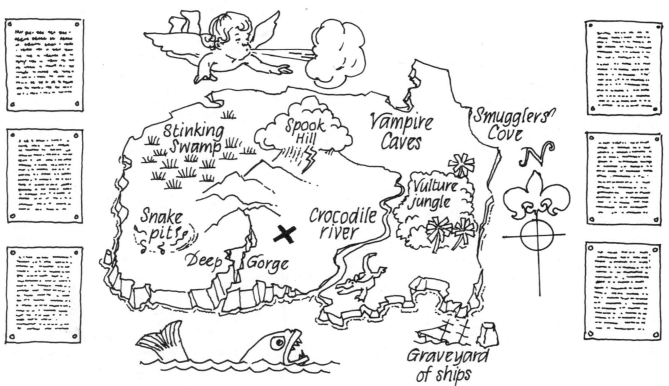

Wool and weaving

Age range
Six plus.

Group size
Small groups or the whole class.

What you need
Sheep's wool, various natural substances to use as dye (such as tea, coffee, onion skins, beetroot), carder, spindle, card, wool, plastic needles, backing paper, hessian in neutral colour or brick wall.

What to do
If possible, go out with the children and collect sheep's wool from the fields and hedges. Keep a little of this on one side for display purposes and wash the rest.

To dye the wool, boil one of the natural substances in water and add the wool. Add more of the substance until you have a darker shade than you need, as the dyed material will dry paler. Hang the wool to dry. Keep a little of each type of dyed wool for display.

The children can try spinning wool using a spindle. This is a tricky job and they will need adult help. Alternatively the children can spin the wool by hand.

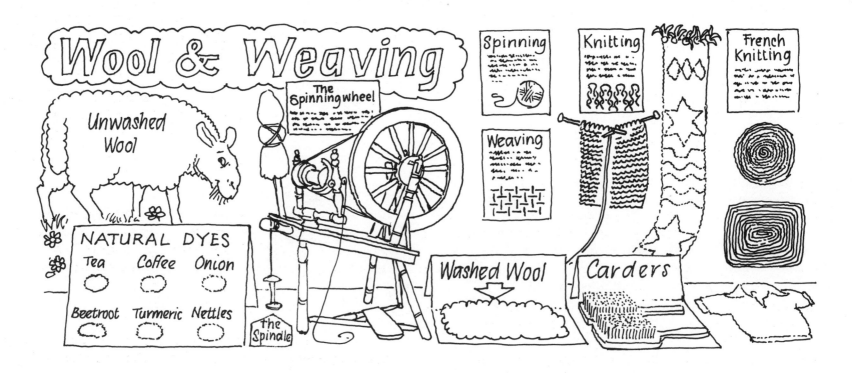

60

When beginning to weave a card can be made by simply wrapping wool around (see figure 1). Alternatively a polystyrene carton may be used (see figure 2).

Figure 1

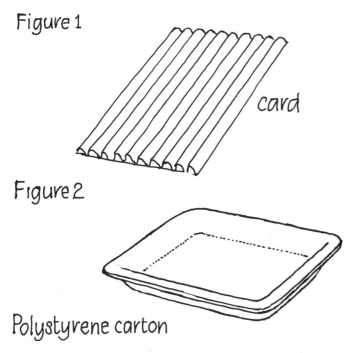

card

Figure 2

Polystyrene carton

The polystyrene carton is easier for young children to handle since there is a gap below the wool and the children have less difficulty in manipulating the needle under and over when weaving. Strips of unspun wool can be included at intervals to give a more interesting texture.

Weaving can also be done on a variety of objects. All that is required is an anchor for the warp and weft.

Branches or twigs from trees make interesting hangers for weaving, and of course the wool can be used for knitting as well.

Display as shown, using the hessian as a drape and small masonry nails to hang things if you use a brick wall.

Crowd scenes

Age range
Six plus.

Group size
Small groups or the whole class.

What you need
Drawing paper, paints, wax crayons, felt-tipped pens, tissue-paper, cold-water paste, scrap materials such as matchboxes, bobbins, wood shavings, cheese boxes, aerosol lids, spent matches, balsa, scraps of yarn and fabric.

What to do
First choose a subject for the scene, such as spectators at a sporting event, a theatre, a circus, the street or the class.

Give each child a piece of paper about the size of a head, then ask them to draw or paint a face to fill the paper completely and cut it out. To give the scene some perspective use graduated sizes of paper, larger ones at the front and smaller ones at the back.

Facial features can be added in a variety of ways using paper sculpture and scrap materials. The children will enjoy creating their own characters. Encourage them to create lots of different ones: men, women and children of all ages and colours. Make bodies for the figures at the front by drawing round a child and sticking clothes made from scraps of material to the cut-out shape.

Choose a dark background and mount the faces so that they are all looking in the same direction if they are spectators. For a street scene they can be looking in all directions. For a circus audience, arrange the faces in a semi-circle facing inwards and use lighter colours to spotlight a section of the crowd. Finally stick or staple the bodies to the background.

Cogs and wheels

Age range
Six plus.

Group size
Whole class.

What you need
Card, thread, fabric, large boxes of various sizes, a range of paints, paper, a collection of cogs, wheels and springs, insides of clocks, photographs or posters of different kinds and uses of cogs and wheels, old toy cars.

What to do

Suspend cog wheel mobiles in front of a draped board and allow the drapes to trail on to a horizontal surface.

Place boxes of different sizes underneath the drapes, the largest ones at the back and the smallest ones at the front, and display the collection of cogs, wheels and springs on the horizontal surfaces.

Get the children to make patterns by printing with cogs and wheels or by dipping the wheels of toy cars in paint and running them over the paper. Display these on the back wall along with the photos and posters.

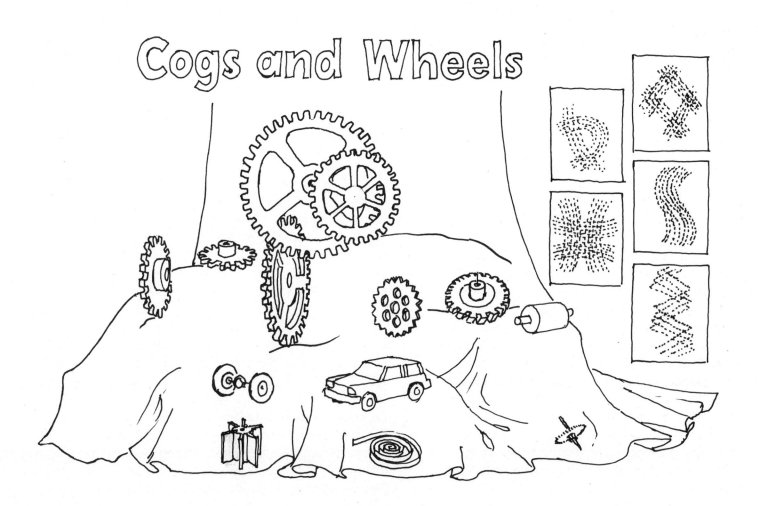

Market stalls

Age range
Any age.

Group size
Small groups, teacher to make canopy.

What you need
Paper,
paint,
transparent wrapping material,
scissors,
adhesive,
card,
felt-tipped pens.

What to do
A row of brightly coloured market stalls can be useful not only as a starter for creative writing or poetry but also for teaching money handling skills to younger children. The stalls can be 2-D or 3-D depending on the amount of space available.

For a 2-D display the stall or barrow can be painted on to a backing sheet with the boxes left empty. The children can then paint apples, oranges, bananas, grapes, lettuces etc, and fill the empty boxes by sticking or stapling the produce in place. The canopy can be painted in red and white stripes and scalloped along the bottom edge. A strip of rolled activity paper folded can make a bracket for the canopy.

If there is enough space, a 3-D market stall can be made quite easily by using a table for the base. Newspaper rods can be made for the upright columns: two long ones for the back and two shorter ones for the

front. Three rods stuck together will give extra strength at each corner. For the horizontal bars, going from corner to corner at the front and back, longer rods will be needed. These can be made from rolled up advertising sheets or, if these are not available, garden canes will do instead. Once the frame is complete, the canopy can be made and stuck in place.

The stall is then ready for selling whatever the children want to: fruit and vegetables, fish, flowers, cakes or toys. The fruit and vegetables can be made from Plasticine or salt dough, and the flowers by sticking tissue-paper flowers on to art straws and putting them in vases. Fish can be made in 3-D by cutting out two identical shapes and padding the middle with crumpled tissue-paper as the two shapes are joined together. The children could either make toys in the same way, or bring in some of their own toys or games to buy and sell on the stall.

Monsters of the deep

Age range
Any age.

Group size
Individuals or pairs.

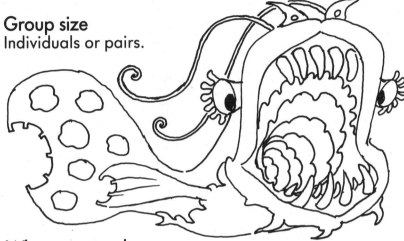

What you need
Large white art paper, powder paints including some fluorescent colours, scraps of material for collage, sponges, green and brown wax crayons, dark green crêpe paper.

What to do
Allow the children to paint their own idea of a sea monster as large as possible (about 80 cm by 40 cm). Let them use the fluorescent paints on some part of the creature and stick on any collage scraps etc. If possible, let them cut out their own monster and stick it up. Curve the paper in 3-D fashion to make the monsters stand out.

For the background use sponges over wax crayon to make a sludgy green-brown wash and wax sea. Leave the background plain instead of wavy, to offset the bright paintings. Use a dark green strip of crêpe paper for an edging if needed.

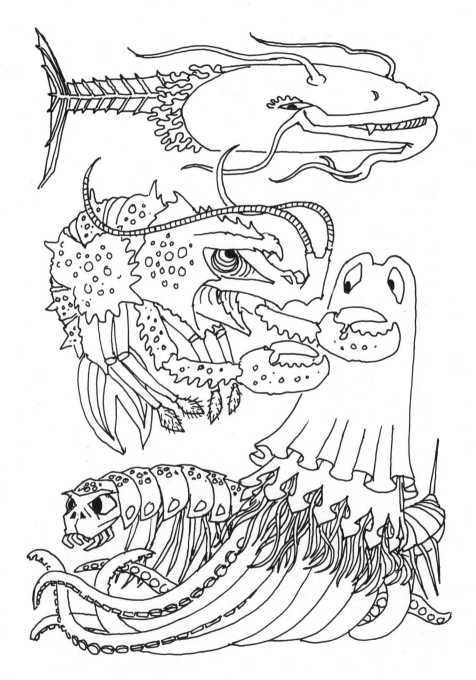

Under-sea world

Age range
Six plus.

Group size
Small groups.

What you need
Backing paper of dark blue or green, sandy-coloured activity paper, white art paper, stiff brown paper, several shades of green activity paper, several shades of green and blue transparent wrapping paper, assorted coloured foil, bits of old jewellery, thick yellow wool, sawdust or shavings, adhesive, green and blue glitter.

What to do
Mount the blue backing paper to the top half of the board for the sea. Cut the right amount of sandy paper for the sea bed, then spread thick patches of adhesive at the front and sprinkle some wood shavings over it. When this is dry, mount it so that it overlaps the blue paper at a slight angle.

Mount a tessallated fish shoal (see page 49) swimming through a transparent wrapping paper weed bank. Slope this to add movement. Draw a mermaid on white paper, and paint the head and body in flesh tones. Cut out fish scales in green and blue foil and stick these on the tail starting from the bottom and overlapping each layer. When it is dry paint the edges of the top side of the tail with adhesive and sprinkle it thickly with green and blue glitter. Stick the hair on in long thick strands from scalp to outer edge, and mount her on the board sitting on a tissue-paper rock.

Draw a treasure chest on art paper and paint it brown, adding gold foil hinges and corners. Cut out jewels in assorted foil and stick these and the 'real' jewels in the opening.

Cut out a boat shape and then cut this into planks. Glue these together slightly overlapping. When it is dry cut out the hole, leaving the bottom plank intact. Staple it to the sea bed allowing the shape to bell out giving a 3-D effect.

To make an octopus, draw and cut out the head and three or four legs in one piece, and cut out the remaining legs separately. Use coloured activity paper for the octopus and stick on foil suckers. Mount the body in the hole in 3-D fashion, staple the legs inside the boat and bend them over the edge, and fix it to wall. Add sea plants in green.

Hospitals

Age range
Display by teacher.

Group size
Whole class.

What you need
One or two flat and narrow boxes covered in blue fabric or paper, blue art paper, white crêpe paper, a large doll in good condition, a teddy bear with a bandaged head, arm and tummy, a white cotton cot blanket, a doll's bed, a dressing-up nurse's uniform, topic books and fiction stories on hospitals and related subjects, adhesive, sticky tape, stapler.

What to do
Cut out, 'Have you been to hospital?' in large lower-case letters from the blue art paper. Cut out a speech bubble in stiff white paper or card and stick on the letters. Display as shown, putting a white paper frill round the boxes. Don't overcrowd the display with books, and make a temporary book-end with a paper-covered house brick.

Vegetables

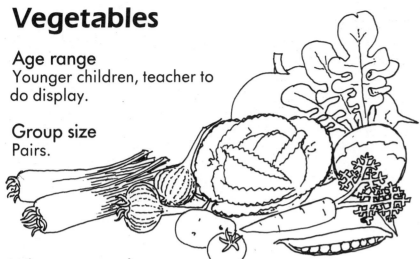

Age range
Younger children, teacher to do display.

Group size
Pairs.

What you need
Advertising sheets or paper 1.5 m square, powder paint, wide brushes or sponges, thick black felt-tipped pen, PVA adhesive.

What to do
Keeping one vegetable per sheet, draw overlapping groups in pencil. Ask the children to paint them, introducing the concept of shading. Allow the paintings to dry thoroughly and then outline each vegetable in thick felt-tipped pen. Without touching the felt-tipped pen, paint carefully with a slightly watered PVA adhesive. This will dry to a sheen and add light tones to the finished painting. Cut out each collection, then choose a backing colour to complement and highlight the painting: for example, brown for carrots, light green for dark green cabbage, yellow for onions, etc.

When stapling the painting to the backing, staple about 5 cm in on one side, allow the sheet to bell out slightly and staple 5 cm in on the other side. Make sure it is positioned centrally on the board. Finish off the board with a crêpe paper frill in a toning colour.

Fantasy castle

Age range
Teacher and any age group for painting, seven plus for flowers, leaves and mounting.

Group size
Two to three people to hang display, children's groups of three to four.

What you need
1.5 m of 2 m corrugated card in beige and white, three advertising sheets or 2 m by 1.5 m news-sheet, two or three shades of green art paper, art paper in assorted colours, crêpe paper in assorted colours, adhesive, stapler, staple gun, scissors, two 2 m canes, assorted paints. To make the castle exactly as described a landing is needed but it can be adapted for use elsewhere.

What to do

Cut the corrugated card as shown with the ridges vertical and fix the canes to the back using a strong PVA adhesive. Calculate the distance from 1 m above the landing handrail to the ceiling and, using strong paper (advertising sheet), make two hanging strips as shown. Get the older children to draw and paint the front and back of the castle, one on each sheet. Stick one on each side of the card, and finish the edges as shown with crêpe paper in a colour to tone or contrast with the castle colour. Cover the edges of the card completely. Firmly fix hanging strips to the top of the roof using staples, and fix the castle to the ceiling by threading strips over the ceiling tile supports. If hanging is not possible, don't paint the back of the castle but cover it with coloured art paper, including a third and fourth cane as shown, and stick it neatly to the landing rail.

Make some origami or tissue-paper flowers in assorted colours and mount each on a circle of art paper in the same colour as the castle edging. Cut assorted lengths of crêpe paper in the same colour as the mounts and staple one end to each mount and the other to the ceiling. Cut out enough leaves to fill each handrail and fix them with sticky tape as shown. Make an assortment of turrets, arrange them in twos and threes within the leaves and stick these to the rail uprights. Hide the tape with a leaf.

The clock men

Age range
Five to seven.

Group size
Small groups with help for younger ones.

What you need
Coloured card,
black activity paper,
paper-fasteners,
felt-tipped pens,
coloured wool.

What to do
Cut out all the pieces from coloured card, apart from the clock hands, and stick them into place as shown. Write the numbers and fit the hands, cut from black activity paper, with a paper-fastener. Hang the clock men as mobiles with coloured wool.

Reading scheme characters

Age range
Five to seven.

Group size
Individuals for pictures, pairs for Plasticine garden objects.

What you need
Activity paper, crayons, white paper, Plasticine.

What to do
Using the reading scheme books for the children to copy from, ask individuals to draw the characters and their homes (most schemes include this element). Get pairs of children to make Plasticine models of items belonging to the characters, then display the characters each with his or her home and belongings.

Christmas scene

Age range
Any age.

Group size
Individuals for each figure, group assembly.

What you need
Cardboard tubes,
scrap material,
corrugated card,
sand.

What to do
Make a variety of figures from cardboard tubes as shown, and two or three trees. Cover the base with sand, and arrange the figures.

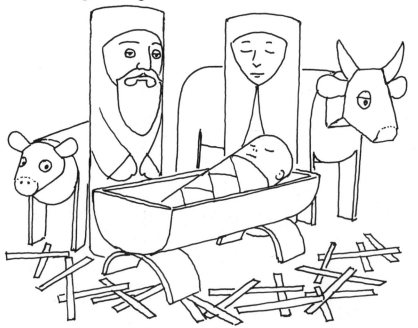

Bonfire night

Age range
Any age.

Group size
Whole class, teacher to fix display.

What you need
Black and grey art paper, white paper, paints, scissors, wax crayons, crêpe paper, thread.

What to do
Ask two or three children to paint the bonfire, with help if necessary. Get the rest of the class to draw the front facing figures and the fireworks. A small group could draw and cut out silhouettes in grey paper. Make a stencil for them to use if necessary. Arrange the figures as you like on the black art paper with the children sticking on their own items. Use crêpe paper to suggest fireworks, varying the colour.

Finish the picture with a frill and hang any written work or vocabulary up as mobiles.

Hallowe'en

Age range
Any age.

Group size
Individuals and small groups.

What you need
Art paper, coloured foil (including green), black crêpe paper, black activity paper, tissue-paper, paints or wax crayons, brightly coloured crêpe paper, art straws.

What to do
A Hallowe'en display can incorporate anything to do with witches. It could centre on a large picture of a witch either flying on her broomstick or stirring her cauldron to make spells.

Witch masks can be made by cutting out a face shape with a pointed chin from any colour art paper.

Fold it down the middle and cut out a jagged mouth.

Cut out a witch's pointed hat from the black activity paper.

Cut two strips of tissue-paper for the witch's hair and make it into long fringes.

Cut out a long pointed witch's nose the same colour as the face, and cut two shiny eyes from the green foil.

Assemble the face but stick the hair on to the face before sticking the hat in place. The hat will help to hide the ends of the hair.

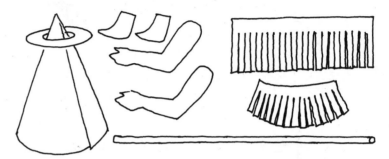

A simple witch mobile can be made from a semicircle of black activity paper. Form this into a cone, then cut out a circle of black card with a hole in the centre and place this over the point of the cone. Now cut two arm shapes and a shape for the face. Take some brightly coloured crêpe paper, fringe it and attach as shown. The children can draw their own witchy faces. The fringe of hair and the face can then be stuck into position.

These witches can be either hung as mobiles with black crêpe paper or folded and pinned to the wall.

Older children can make a pumpkin mask. Get them to draw their own or use a stencil, cut them out and decorate them with wax crayons, or make prints with paint. Display these against coloured foil.

Finally use an art straw and some black activity paper to make the broom. Fringe the paper, wind it around the art straw and glue it into position. Push the finished broom through the witch's cloak.

These can be hung as mobiles or stood in a group as witches on a hillside.

Red Indians

Age range
Six plus.

Group size
Small groups or whole class.

What you need
Cardboard boxes, card, adhesive, scissors, staples, sticky tape, tissue-paper, wool, paints, wax crayons, felt-tipped pens, feathers, sand, paper, peas, washing-up liquid bottles, biscuit tin.

What to do
Explore all aspects of Red Indian life long ago. You can look at wigwams, the bright clothes, the feather head-dresses, the totem-poles etc.

Children could make a totem-pole from different-sized boxes placed on top of each other and painted with animal and bird faces. Cut out feathers from activity paper to decorate the pole.

Young children will enjoy dressing up as Indians. They could make Indian headbands quite simply with a strip of card to fit round the head. Decorate using real feathers or paper ones. Use sticky tape to fasten them to the card. Decorate the front of the band with a design using wax crayon or felt-tipped pens.

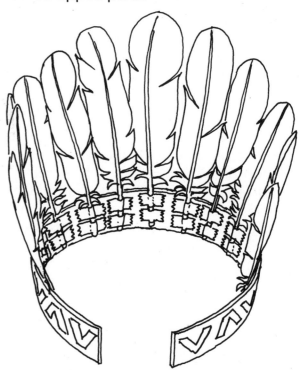

The children could find out about the way in which Red Indians hunted and fished, about the work of the squaws, how they gathered nuts and berries in burden baskets. These are also easy to make and could form part of your display.

Take a piece of card, 30 cm by 60 cm, and join the ends. Cut a circle for the bottom which is larger than the diameter of the tube. Cut the edges of the circle so that they can be folded up and stuck inside the tube.

Next take a strip of cloth or paper and fasten this to the side of the basket. This strip is worn round the head as illustrated.

Indian masks are another good addition to the display. These can be as scary and colourful as the child's imagination allows.

Shields are also colourful and very bright and there are lots of different designs of birds, fishes etc which can be used.

Red Indians believed in magic and they made patterns in the sand to drive away evil spirits. Re-create these patterns by putting adhesive into a squeezy washing-up liquid bottle. Draw a pattern on a piece of card and then trace the pattern with the adhesive. Sprinkle sand on to the pattern and let the adhesive dry. Shake off any excess sand.

Collect these items together to make a classroom display to show how Red Indians lived long ago.

Make musical instruments such as tom-toms and rattles. Rattles can be made quite simply by putting dried peas or beans in a washing-up liquid bottle. Mix powder paint with PVA adhesive then paint any decoration on to the bottle surface. A tom-tom can be made from an old biscuit tin.

The jungle

Age range
Six plus.

Group size
Small groups or whole class.

What you need
Card, paints, wax crayons, adhesive, scissors, stapler, tissue-paper, crêpe paper, activity paper, newspapers, garden netting, wool, feathers, foil, cotton, coloured acetate film, papier mâché, chicken wire, cardboard boxes.

What to do
Paint a jungle background of leaves and dense undergrowth. Add some large leaves cut out from activity paper, in various shades of green. Make large exotic flowers from tissue-paper and place these around the base of the display.

The display can be made more 3-D by trailing leaves and creepers from the ceiling immediately in front of the wall or the surface you are using. Garden netting can be used to extend the display at the base.

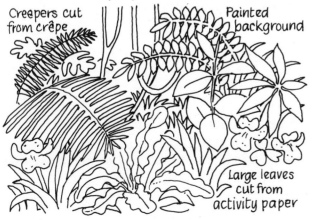

Creepers cut from crêpe

Painted background

Large leaves cut from activity paper

Get the children to paint or collage the many different kinds of creatures which can be found in the jungle. Large exotic birds can be hung from the ceiling or pinned or stapled to the top of the display. Concertina or spiral snakes can hang down from the trees. Beautiful insects or spiders can fly about or be crawling on the trees and leaves. Finally some of the larger jungle dwellers can be painted and cut out or models made to stand in front of the display.

Birds can be easily made. Cut out a body template in card for younger children. Older children can create their own. Cut out wing shapes in the same way and decorate with tissue-paper and wool, brightly-coloured feathers and foil strips to give added sparkle.

←Cut

←Cut

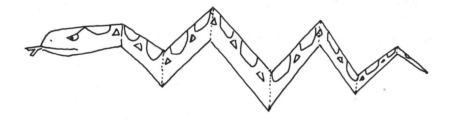

The insects can be made by cutting the body shape from black card then making wings from coloured acetate film.

By making the body symmetrical, the insect can be cut quickly from a piece of folded card. To make the wings pinch a rectangle of coloured acetate film in the middle and staple to the body.

The snakes and crawling insects are easily cut out and decorated using paint or wax crayons. Younger children will particularly enjoy making these.

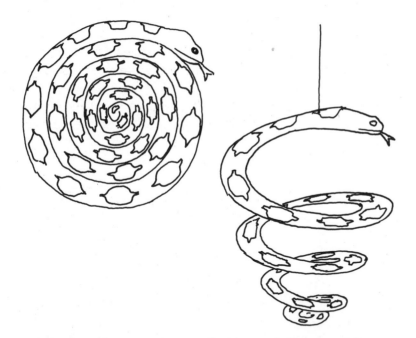

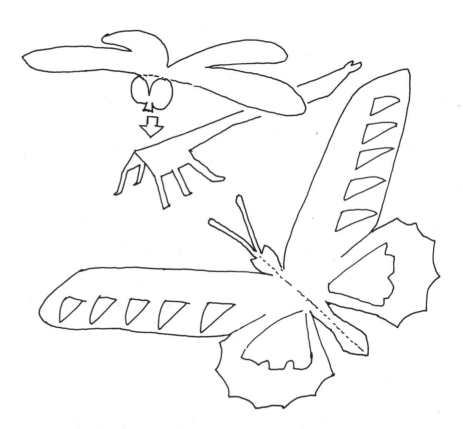

Spiral snakes can be cut from card. Draw a 10 cm diameter circle and then draw a spiral from the centre outwards. Add an oval shaped head, decorate, then carefully cut the snake out by cutting along the spiral line. Finally make a small hole in the snakes head and suspend it with cotton.

They can be suspended in front of the display to give the impression of flight.

The crawling insects are cut out in the same way and painted with bright or fluorescent colours.

Cavemen

Age range
Six plus.

Group size
Whole class.

What you need
Rolls of wallpaper lining paper, paint, stapler and a range of materials to make various artefacts.

What to do
A corner of the classroom could be converted to a cave dwelling. Large advertising sheets are ideal for this but if these are not available then long strips of wallpaper lining paper can be painted with a brown or grey colour wash and then crumpled up and stapled over the corner to make an arch.

The larger animals can be painted as 2-D or painted on card and stuck to the side of a box which will allow them to stand in front of the display. They can also be modelled in various ways using rolled up newspapers, chicken wire with papier mâché or with cardboard boxes and odds and ends of junk material.

The children will enjoy using the cave dwelling for imaginative play and this could possibly lead to the development of drama and be an ideal stimulus for a topic on cavemen as the comparisons between their life and ours are noticed.

The display could grow with paintings and drawings of the different aspects of life. The children could even try to make some of the many different types of artefacts using natural materials such as stones, animal skin, sticks and clay.

Dinosaurs

Age range
Six plus.

Group size
Whole class.

What you need
Collection of posters,
fossils,
pencils,
paint,
sticky tape,
tissue-paper,
Plasticine,
papier mâché,
paper spills,
models of dinosaurs,
pictures of dinosaur eggs.

What to do
Collect posters and pictures of the many different kinds of dinosaurs. Get the children to draw or paint pictures of the vegetarian dinosaurs and the meat-eating ones like *Tyrannosaurus Rex*. Look at the different habitats they lived in such as on land and in the sea.

Look at the evidence showing that dinosaurs lived. Try and make a collection of fossils. Look at the skeletons of dinosaurs and try to arrange a visit to a museum which has suitable skeletons.

Models of different kinds of dinosaurs can be constructed from Plasticine or papier mâché. Skeletons could be constructed using rolled up paper spills. There are many dinosaur toys and these can be used to create a landscape or diorama.

Try to find pictures of fossilised dinosaur eggs. These could lead on to creative writing . . . 'The mysterious egg' or 'The giant footprint'.

Look for animals descended from dinosaurs that are still alive today like the crocodile.

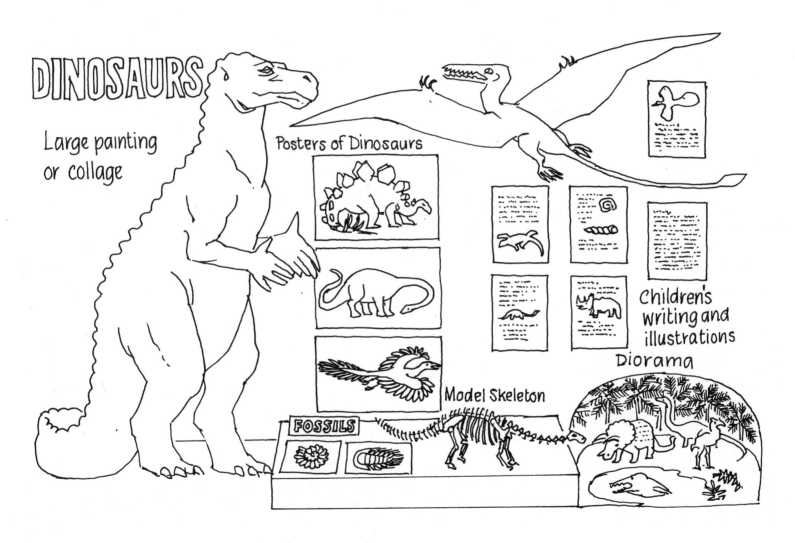

DINOSAURS

Large painting or collage

Posters of Dinosaurs

Children's writing and illustrations

Diorama

Model Skeleton

FOSSILS

Time

Age range
Six plus.

Group size
Whole class.

What you need
Card, paper, adhesive, paper-fasteners, felt-tipped pens, pencils, paints, scissors, collection of many different kinds of time pieces.

What to do
Draw or paint a large circle (1 m diameter) to be used as the clock face. Cut out numbers from black activity paper. This clock will form the centre piece of the display. Cut out the hands from black card and use a paper-fastener to fix them to the clock. This can now be used as a large visual aid.

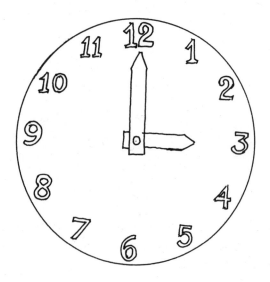

Give the children a template (see page 125) or a printed sheet with a clock face on it so that they can put the numbers in the correct position and make their own clocks. They can move the hands to the correct time when requested.

The children can then draw or paint pictures of the different things they do at certain times of the day, eg getting up, having breakfast, going to school, having playtime, having lunch, ending with going to bed.

To extend the display, illustrations of the seasons, days of the week, months of the year can be included.

Finally, an area can be set aside to display the different things used to calculate the passage of time, eg egg-timers, candle clocks, rockers, sundials, water clocks, and as many different kinds of watch and clock as the children can collect.

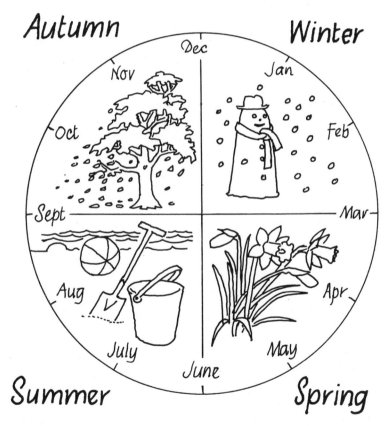

Seasons Clock

Knights and castles

Age range
Six plus.

Group size
Groups or whole class.

What you need
Paint, paper, adhesive, staples, card, boxes of various sizes, foil, silver spray paint.

What to do
To begin the topic have a discussion about surnames to see if there are any that might lend themselves to easy illustrations eg Walker, Miller, Cooper, Smith, Farmer etc. The children could make a flag or shield and decorate it with their own coat of arms.

They could look out for institutions in their own locality which bear a coat of arms such as banks, local authorities, firms or schools.

The children can try to find out as much as possible about knights and their armour and the code of conduct and the work of squires and pages.

As part of the display the children could try to construct a full size suit of armour from card and boxes covered with silver foil or sprayed with silver paint.

Most of the knights lived in castles. A good idea for a display of children's writing on this topic might be to do a large painting of a castle to cover one whole wall and display the writing on various parts of the castle.

Children could make models of castles from large boxes as the main structures and smaller boxes as the towers and out buildings. The crenellations can be cut out from card and stuck on.

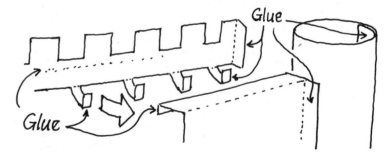

The castle could be on a small scale to accommodate toy soldiers or on a larger scale so that children could use it for imaginative role play.

One aspect of life in a castle was the feasting and merry-making. As part of the display you could set a table for a feast. Try to find out about the kinds of food that would have been eaten eg strange things such as boar's heads or swans. If the king was visiting the castle they might even eat a peacock.

They drank from goblets and were entertained by minstrels who sang songs and jesters who told stories and made people laugh.

Knights seemed to spend a lot of their time jousting and there are many myths about the killing of dragons and the rescuing of damsels in distress. Writing and paintings to illustrate this would further add to the display.

Special occasions

There are certain occasions which demand a one- or two-day display. These need to be easily set up, possibly movable (eg at dinner-time), highly informative or directive and, of course, of the highest display standards to have the required impact to its audience.

Most of these displays will be for parents so there may be a need to use more complex language in directions or labels. In multi-ethnic areas a considerable percentage of parents may not read English, so it is essential to enlist the help of bilingual members of the community to help in the production of notices in the mother tongue of the main ethnic groups.

'Special' occasions where you might want to have a display are: pre-school meetings, PTA events, parent/governor meetings, school holiday arrangements or adverts, school fairs, school performances (plays, assemblies, festivals), parents' evenings or parent-teacher consultations, book displays or sales, doctor or dentist visits, police visits (road safety etc) and, sports day.

First of all make a note of what information you want to pass on and what equipment or other items you want to show. Decide whether you will need directions, such as 'This way', if there is to be a meeting. If so, you will have to provide adequate seating arranged in such a way that your display items can be seen, especially if they are needed as visual aids during a talk.

If the main display boards and sites are in use during the time of the special display you'll probably want to use temporary boards unless it is to last any length of time.

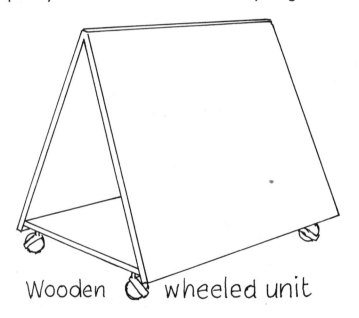

Wooden wheeled unit

There are several purpose-built free standing display-boards and wooden wheeled units on the market.

Good old corrugated card can be enlisted for temporary use if a wall anchorage is available, as it is difficult to move in a long section. A temporary display can be pinned on to the card and stood in front of an existing display.

Painting easels can be used to support colourful art paper on which you can display information, directions and so on.

Dining tables can be enlisted as base units for quick displays of equipment, such as books, holiday clothes, sports equipment, uniforms etc. Notices can be fixed to chair backs or mounted on the tables. For school fairs where crowds are expected, notices need to be high up so they can be seen. It might be possible to put these easels on tables but make sure that they can't be easily knocked off.

The main hall curtains will provide a very handy temporary surface. Art paper can be carefully pinned to the closed curtains. Use a complementary colour or a stark contrast.

A quick display surface can also be made from a clothes horse and some old but tasteful curtains draped over it. Notices can also be pinned to window curtains.

PE mat storage units covered with a curtain or with frieze paper stuck to them provide a good large base. PE benches can be used sideways on top of stage blocks as poster mounts or as a shelf for displaying 3-D items.

If possible, site temporary displays in front of a neutral backing like a bare wall, closed curtains, or existing displays covered with corrugated card.

PE mat unit

Cloth or paper

Items cut out and pinned or stuck on backing

Card or stiff paper

sticky tape rolls behind

Don't forget to make all directional labelling very large and bold and put it in prominent positions. Use bold colours and large lettering in a stark contrast – white on black, red on white etc. Remember that pale colours, like yellow, green, pink etc, are difficult to read at a distance. Try unusual shapes to attract attention. You need to influence people's movements so the lettering needs to be more than purely decorative.

Get the children to help with the signs. Younger children can draw round large letter stencils and colour them in with wax crayons, felt-tipped pens or paints (see photocopiable pages 107 to 116). Edge these with thick black felt-tipped pen when they are dry.

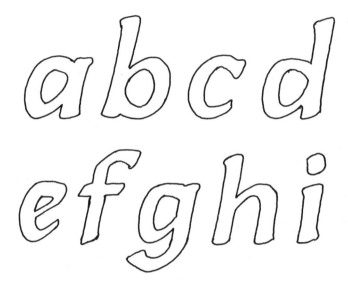

Rounded block letters are surprisingly easy to do. Older children can master them quite quickly. Use a pencil for the first draft and draw guidelines with a ruler. Colour in and edge the letters with pen as before.

If your meeting is in the school hall and you need several display tables, site them in front and to the sides of the audience so that you can refer to them as they are sitting down.

Leave plenty of space round tables and away from chairs to allow for traffic, and don't forget to leave all fire exits unblocked and clearly visible.

A school holiday display

Age range
Teacher and older children to mount and display.

Group size
Three to four.

What you need
About 4 m corrugated card, stapler, pins, latex adhesive, white art paper, an A4-sized ring-binder, A4-sized coloured card, clear sticky-back plastic, thick black marker pens (½ cm and 1 cm size), two flat boxes or display stands, two toning curtains, items of equipment and souvenirs from holidays.

What to do
Display as shown, fixing card on either side of an existing display if this is to be a temporary one. Involve the children in mounting the photos and cutting out letters for the title.

Make a photographic record which can later be stored and displayed as a photo album. Children love looking through photographs of events at school and albums are a good way of displaying them. Each album can contain different items, such as school holidays, trips, events in school, children's work etc.

To make the album mount the photos on A4 card, preferably each single event (ie each holiday or trip) on its own colour. Include captions, children's names and dates, so that in effect you are compiling an historical record. When advertising next year's holiday you can display highlights of the last one.

You can double mount these cards on to large sheets of white art paper and then fix them to the card backing. Use sticky tape to fix the card to the paper and pins to fix the sheets to the corrugated card. When the display is finished, gently remove the sticky tape and after punching holes, transfer the cards to your folder. Photos make good cover subjects for the folder, especially if you choose a funny one.

Print the title and the year and cover the folder with clear sticky-back plastic to protect it. Use coloured card for the backing sheet on the cover as it keeps the colour better than art paper when exposed to the light for long periods.

Parents' association spring dance

Age range
Children can help with art work.

Group size
Whole class.

What you need
Assorted coloured card and activity paper, cartridge paper, adhesive, felt-tipped pens, paints, stapler, scissors, tissue-paper, crêpe paper, sticky tape, corrugated card, one large basket such as a dog basket, enough straw to fill it, prizes, stage blocks or other staging, tables, chairs, bar equipment, and other equipment for entertaining.

What to do
Make advertising posters in the shape of an Easter bunny or an egg. Ask the children to decorate or colour them.

Make information posters with a seasonable flavour by drawing bunny shapes on a large white card or cartridge paper using a thick black felt-tipped pen. Draw the bunny to suit the subject.

NB: Keep all fire exit notices on plain shapes in regulation colours.

Make a welcoming poster for the entrance hall. Cut out a large piece of card in the shape of an Easter egg (at least 1 m tall). Cut out the lettering from activity paper. Paint the egg in a spring-like base colour such as yellow and paint on patterns or decorate it using tissue-paper flowers and a crêpe paper bow. Fasten the egg to the back of a chair using sticky tape. This can then be stood by the hall door or on a table which the doorman is using to collect tickets.

Display the raffle prizes in a seasonal way by filling a large dog basket with straw and placing the prizes in it. Mount the basket on a table in the entrance hall, tilting the basket a little forward by raising the back on a box.

Decorate the bar by cutting out eight to ten Easter eggs out of assorted activity paper. Decorate each with patterns in activity paper and cut out the word 'bar' in black letters approximately 40 cm high. Stick patterns and letters to the eggs and then staple them around the top of the bar area.

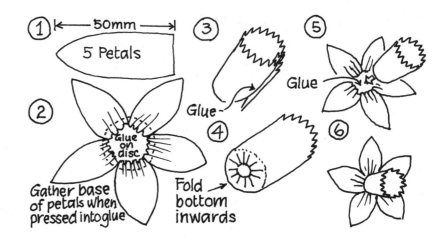

You could decorate the stage for the disco. Make some very large daffodils and some Easter eggs to form an arch over the back of the stage area. To make the daffodils cut out 50 cm long petals in yellow crêpe paper. Make three flowers with five petals each. Cut out three discs of 15 cm diameter from thick corrugated card. Cut out three pieces of bright orange crêpe paper, 20 cm by 50 cm, zig-zag one side of each. Stick the pieces together as shown.

Arrange the stage as illustrated. Mount the decorations on a backing of black corrugated card or on the hall curtains if the stage is arranged near them. You could leave these decorations up in the school hall during the spring term. Cut strips of pale green crêpe to hang down as shown.

The school play

Age range
All ages can help with the special art work.

Group size
Small groups.

What you need
Assorted collage materials, assorted activity paper, white paper, two art easels, stapler, staple gun, scissors, tissue-paper, sticky tape, adhesive, paints, black felt-tipped pens.

What to do
Your school play may be a once or twice a year event which needs a lot of extra display work apart from the scenery involved in the play itself. The extra display items may only be needed for the times of the performance, but it may be possible to keep two items on view for a longer period. The scenery will probably be needed during rehearsals and so will have a long life and you can make a welcoming display using the play characters which can be sited in the entrance hall.

If you have room, each class in the school can do a painting or a collage of one of the major scenes or one of the characters in the play. Over the entrance to the hall itself, make an arch of 'scenery' which the visitors will have to pass under such as into the Land of Oz if you are doing 'The Wizard of Oz'.

Using large card or corrugated card cut out two of the main characters to be sentries. Make them life-size to give impact. Paint and collage them. For 'The Wizard of Oz', you could use a rainbow arch, for 'Snow White' an arch of forest trees, for Cinderella stars and pumpkins etc. The rainbow arch is made by painting a rainbow on a 3 m × 1 m piece of paper and then waving the paper as it is stapled to the wall. Large flowers can be made from tissue-paper and arranged as shown.

Programmes

10p

PHOTOGRAPHS
35p OF THE CAST
each

The Cast

Black paper

Easel

Hall

Writing black on white paper

HAVE YOU SEEN OUR VIDEO OF THE WIZARD OF OZ only 50p book now!

Easel

97

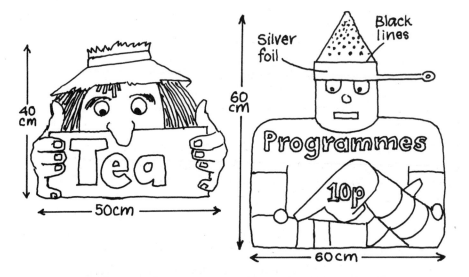

For the performance itself you could make further displays. Photos of the cast, double mounted on a large backing sheet could be displayed. Choose the same colour backing sheet for each of the notices in this small area. Mount the notices on art easels or on chair backs mounted on tables to be at eye-level. Write any information on white paper in black felt-tipped pen and mount this on the backing sheet. These notices can be shaped to add interest. Make sure all fire exit notices are the regulation colour and size.

Sports day

Age range
Seven plus to help on the posters, any age to help with layout of equipment.

Group size
Twos on posters, small groups for other jobs.

What you need
Assorted crêpe paper, balloons, sticky tape, stapler, staple gun, large coloured felt-tipped pens, paints, large letter stencils (see pages 107–116), clear sticky-back plastic, large white and coloured art paper, white card, fluorescent card, mobile display cards or painting easels, two to four rounders posts and stands, tables, skittles (if needed), finishing line, sports equipment (hoops, balls, ropes, batons, etc), prize cards and/or prizes, large, plain, neutral coloured curtain, scraps of bright material, assorted coloured felt, sewing cottons, length of 2 cm dowel (width of curtain), garden canes.

What to do

Get the older children to design posters for display in local shops etc. You could have a competition to decide the best design and then photocopy as many as you need. These 'master copies' can then be coloured in by the children. Or you can simply use all the posters produced. Use large stencils for the heading and let the children write in other details.

Directional arrows can be placed where needed around the school to show visitors to the field, toilets, refreshments etc. Cut out medium weight fluorescent card

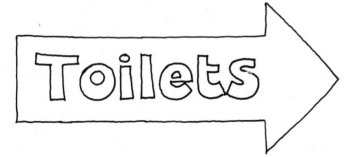

and cover with clear sticky-back plastic to protect them from damp weather and to keep them fresh for subsequent years and events.

Make several signs for facilities to mount near the arrows and cover these in clear sticky-back plastic. Write in clear print using large felt-tipped pens. Outline the edge in black felt-tipped pen.

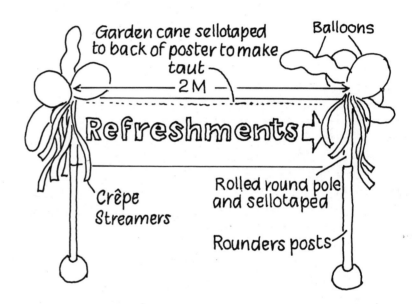

Make large posters using the large stencils in this book (see pages 107 to 116) to write information such as refreshments, teas, school name, Our Sports Day 1988 etc. Colour using paints or felt-tipped pens. Outline the letters in black felt-tipped pen. Decorate and cover with clear sticky-back plastic for reuse next year. Mount on a wall or leave free-standing by using rounders posts as support.

Make a school banner. Use a plain curtain as the base. Draw the design on paper first, then cut out items in paper and position on to the curtain. Next, cut out items in felt and sew into place. Decorative items such as flowers can be stuck on using a latex adhesive or stitched in place to give a 3-D effect. Machine round the edge of the curtain before starting and include a hem at the top through which the dowel can pass.

For carrying – rest between 2 nails on baton and tape into position with electrical tape.

Fix rope to bottom to prevent flapping.

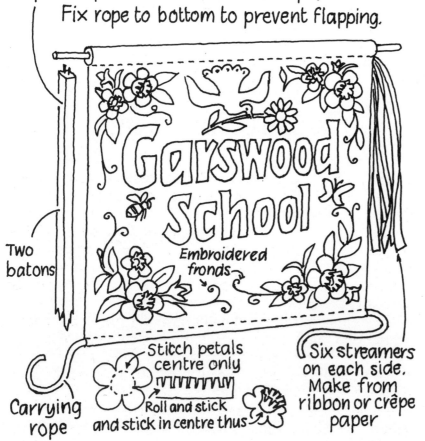

Two batons

Garswood School

Embroidered fronds

Carrying rope

Stitch petals centre only

Roll and stick and stick in centre thus

Six streamers on each side. Make from ribbon or crêpe paper

Bunting can be hung on the school walls or along fencing. Using scraps of very bright material, cut out triangles, 15 cm×25 cm×25 cm and machine the short edge to 2 cm wide cotton tape.

Mobile display board

Programme
1 Hop skip jump
2 Running
3 Egg & spoon
4 3-legged
5 Fancy dress

1M

Have the children design a decorative edging for a typewritten programme showing the order of events. Photocopy this for distribution at the gate as spectators enter. Using large art paper the teacher could write out a larger version to be placed near the start for staff, children or visitors to refer to. Mount on to a large display board or an easel. Use thin plastic decorating sheets to cover if the weather is damp.

The pre-school parents' meeting

Age range
This is done by the teacher but older children can help 'man' the various stands. Infants needed for paintings.

Group size
Whole class.

What you need
Assorted activity paper, scissors, stapler, adhesive, black felt-tipped pens, paints, letter stencils (see pages 107 to 116), roll of corrugated card, clear sticky-back plastic, sticky tape, tables.

What to do
When new parents visit school they like to see children's work, particularly painting and writing so why not show

White paper

Black pen or cut out letters

Welcome to our school
say our reception children

Cut outs from children's work

corrugated cardboard

them some. If your pre-school meeting is planned for the summer term it may be possible to arrange the display in the entrance hall so that this special work can go there. If not it will look equally impressive mounted on painting easels in the main hall or on a long roll of corrugated

card on the stage behind your speakers. Site your stage away from the existing hall art work and stand the roll of card on it.

Reception children of the present year can each paint a self portrait which can be cut out and then all mounted as a class portrait. A simple message can be put above this. Cut letters from black paper and mount on to a colour to tone with the card.

Older infants can paint pictures of people who work in school and these can be mounted on the same colour activity paper and then on corrugated card or on easels at the side of the stage. This will provide the speaker with a useful visual aid when introducing staff. The children could also write a short piece about each person's role in school. Label the pictures with the child's name, age and year to give parents a general guideline. Don't forget to label who the portrait is. Mount the pictures using sticky tape then they can easily be transferred to a classroom after the meeting.

Schools vary but six information tables at a parent's introduction meeting on the following topics are a good idea:
• Books recommended for parents (eg *Ready for School*, Scholastic Publications Ltd).
• Workbooks for children — recommended books and books for sale.
• Booking point for pre-school visits.
• Check point for child's birth certificate.
• Collection point for school's contract form.
• Collection point for school's information booklet.

Make sure that these tables are clearly visible so that you can refer to them during the meeting. For this reason they need to be towards the front yet at the sides of the hall and well spaced so that parents can visit them conveniently.

Label them clearly. Cut out large letters in black paper and mount on a variety of activity paper. Cover these with clear sticky-back plastic to keep them clean and tidy for subsequent years.

Harvest festival

Age range
Children to help with art work and display of food.

Group size
Small groups.

What you need
Assorted activity paper, assorted tissue-paper, crêpe paper, adhesive, scissors, stapler, paints, wax crayons, black felt-tipped pens, sponge, assorted baskets, bowls, corrugated card, cardboard boxes to add height to display, three bales of hay or straw, assorted drapes of autumn colours, dried grasses, fresh flowers, vases, fruit and vegetables and other food.

What to do
Advertise the event if you want to invite parents or local old age pensioners. You could have a competition to design the best invitation card. This design could be photocopied and then coloured by the children. Include a separate reply strip if required. Large versions of the invitation could become a poster for the notice-board.

If your school is large and has a maze of corridors to

the main hall you may need a few directional labels for your visitors. It may be best to use white labels with large black felt-tipped pen lettering for older people whose eyesight may be poor.

Decide on the place for the main display and position

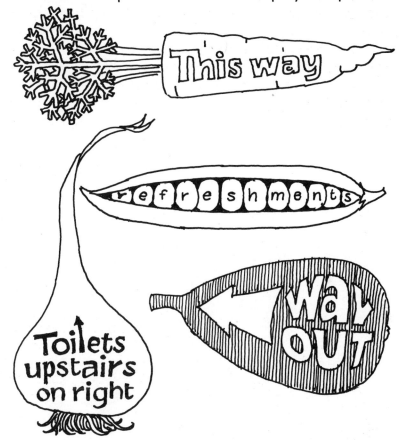

any stage blocks in a curve if possible, against the wall. If you are displaying against the hall curtains and they are a suitable colour you will not need any other backing. If not, use a curtain or activity paper of an autumn colour to provide this backing. Mount the backing.

Make a heading poster by using a 2 m piece of paper,

103

cut into a curve and painted if necessary. A sponge and two tones of paint gives a good effect. Using the large stencils in this book (see pages 107 to 116) and a suitable colour of activity paper, cut out the title, eg 'Our Harvest'. A crêpe paper frill will finish the edge off. Use leaf prints of very large leaves, cut out to decorate the ends. Fruits drawn with very heavy wax crayons and cut out will also add colour to the ends.

Decorate the front of the display box with a crêpe paper frill and cover the top of the box with paper too if necessary.

Now you will be ready to build up the display of food. Position the base boxes in a pyramid with the highest point at the centre back of the display, or use the bales of straw for this purpose.

Make sets of foods of the same colour and starting with the biggest pile, arrange these foods in baskets and bowls in a spread all over the display. Now fit in groups

Cut in a curve shape

Harvest time

Our harvest of plenty

of items of different colours but make sure that you have for instance a little red on both sides to give a colour balance.

Finally have a vase of flowers centre top and fit in dried grasses and other flowers at the sides and back to give height.

If you can decorate your entrance hall in an autumn theme, including work from all the age groups in school all the better. It can be filled with topic work on food,

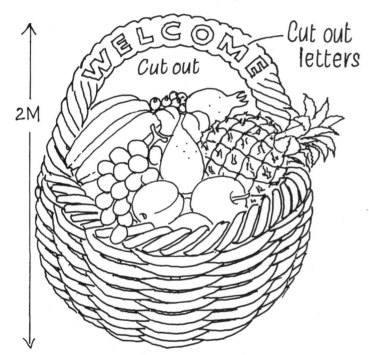

farming, other lands and allied topics. A welcoming poster especially for the harvest will add to the special quality of the event.

Use a 2 m×1.5 m piece of corrugated card. Cut out an oval and draw a basket shape on this. Next, using the smooth side as the front, cut out a shape as shown and paint the basket part of the shape in browns and yellows.

Paint and cut out a large selection of fruit and vegetables and some leaves. Leaf prints will look especially good. Children from reception onward can paint the food and leaves. Cut out the paintings and glue them on to the middle of the basket, but bend them to give a 3-D effect. Stick the card to the back of a chair and position it as close to the hall entrance as possible where all visitors will see it.

Most schools like to show children the difference between our harvest and that of the third world. You can highlight this contrast by displaying a small simple bowl of rice on a white cloth on a separate plinth.

Reproducible material

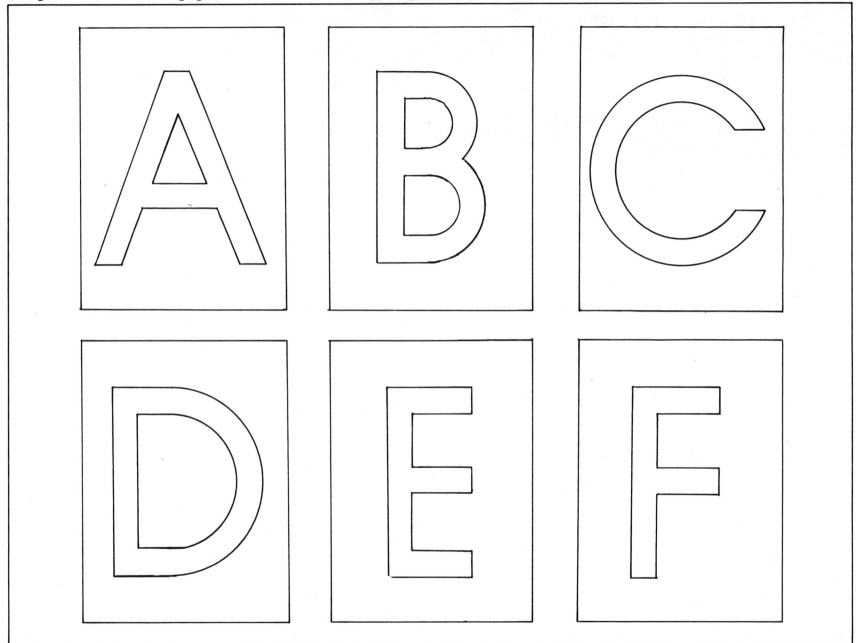

This page may be photocopied for use in the classroom and should not be declared in any return in respect of any photocopying licence.

Alphabet – lower case, see pages 19, 38, 92, 98, 101 and 104

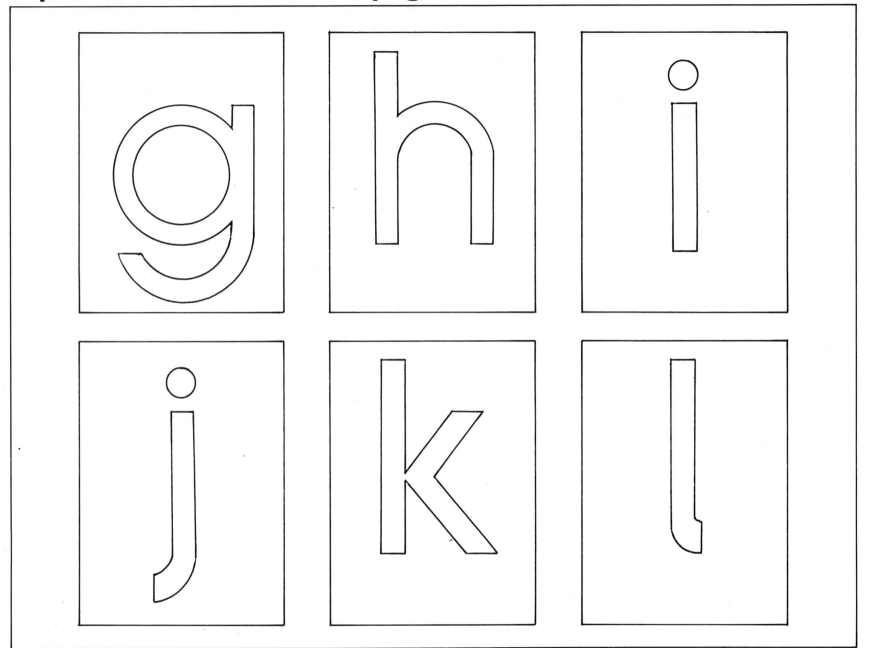

Alphabet – lower case, see pages 19, 38, 92, 98, 101 and 104

Alphabet – lower case, see pages 19, 38, 92, 98, 101 and 104

Sample alphabets, see page 21

abcdefgghijklmnopqqrstu

vwxyyz 1234567890?!"&

ABCDEFGHIJKLMN

OPQRSTUVWXYZ

Flourishes can be added. A B M etc.

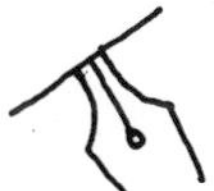

45° nib angle to the paper constant except where reverse diagonal in capitals occurs. eg AKMNVWY&Z. Adopt the vertical thus: for these strokes.

Turn nib on left hand corner for hair line serifs

paper

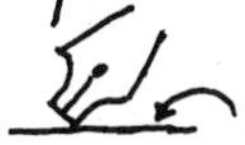

Sample alphabets, see page 21

A B C D E F G H I
J K L M N O P Q
R S T U V W X Y Z

a b c d e f g h i j
k l m n o p q r s t
u v w x y z 1 2 3
4 5 6 7 8 9 0 *nib angle*
Expanded sans serif

Sample alphabets, see page 21

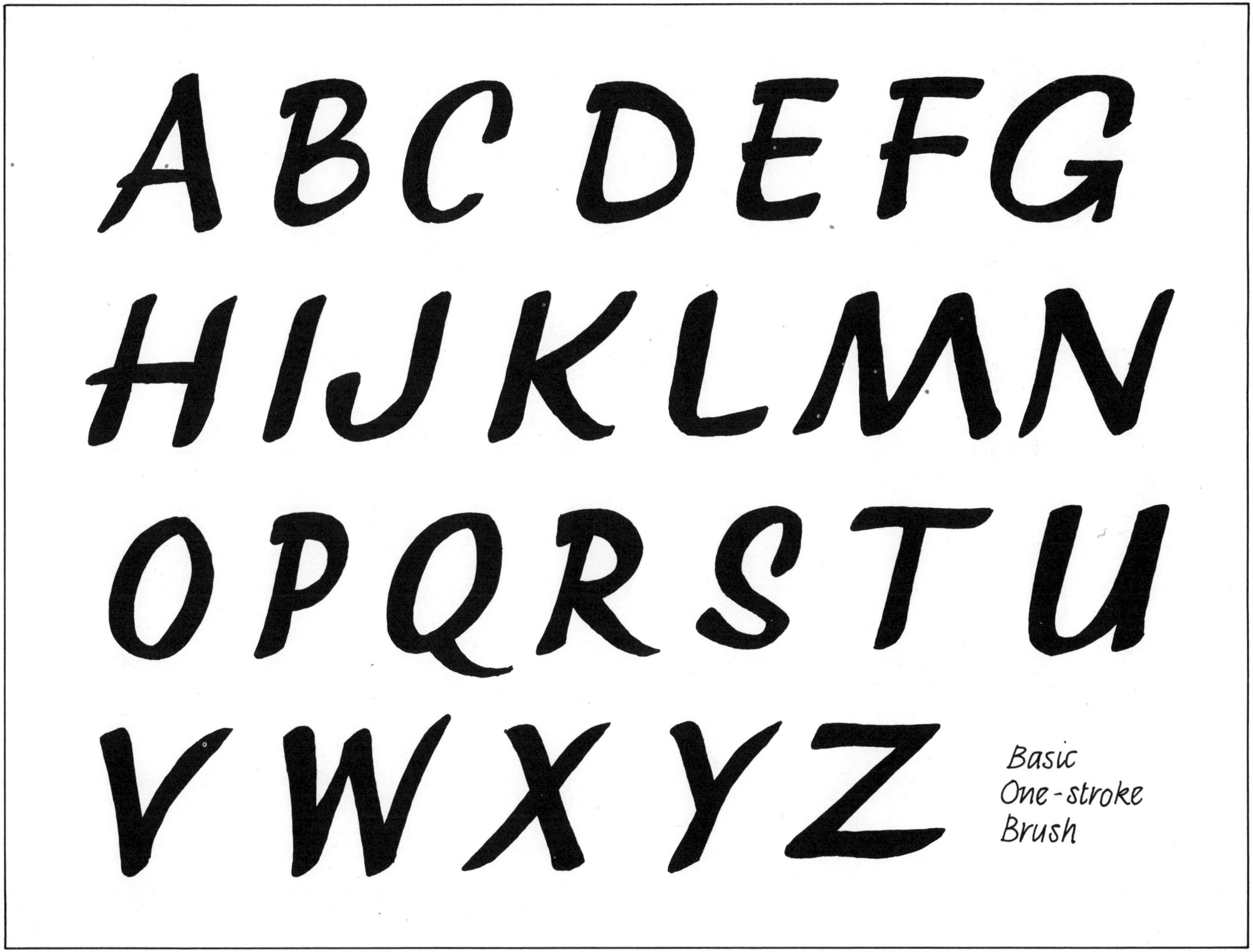

A B C D E F G
H I J K L M N
O P Q R S T U
V W X Y Z
Basic
One-stroke
Brush

Sample alphabets, see page 21

First sketch in the skeleton, then surround with freely drawn shape.

Basic sausage alphabet

Sample alphabets, see page 21

abcdefgghijklm
nib angle
nopqrstuvwxyz
1234567890&?!"
ABCDEFGHIJKL
MNOPQRSTUV
WXYZ
Basic round hand serifs
1 2 3
avoid wavy horizontals

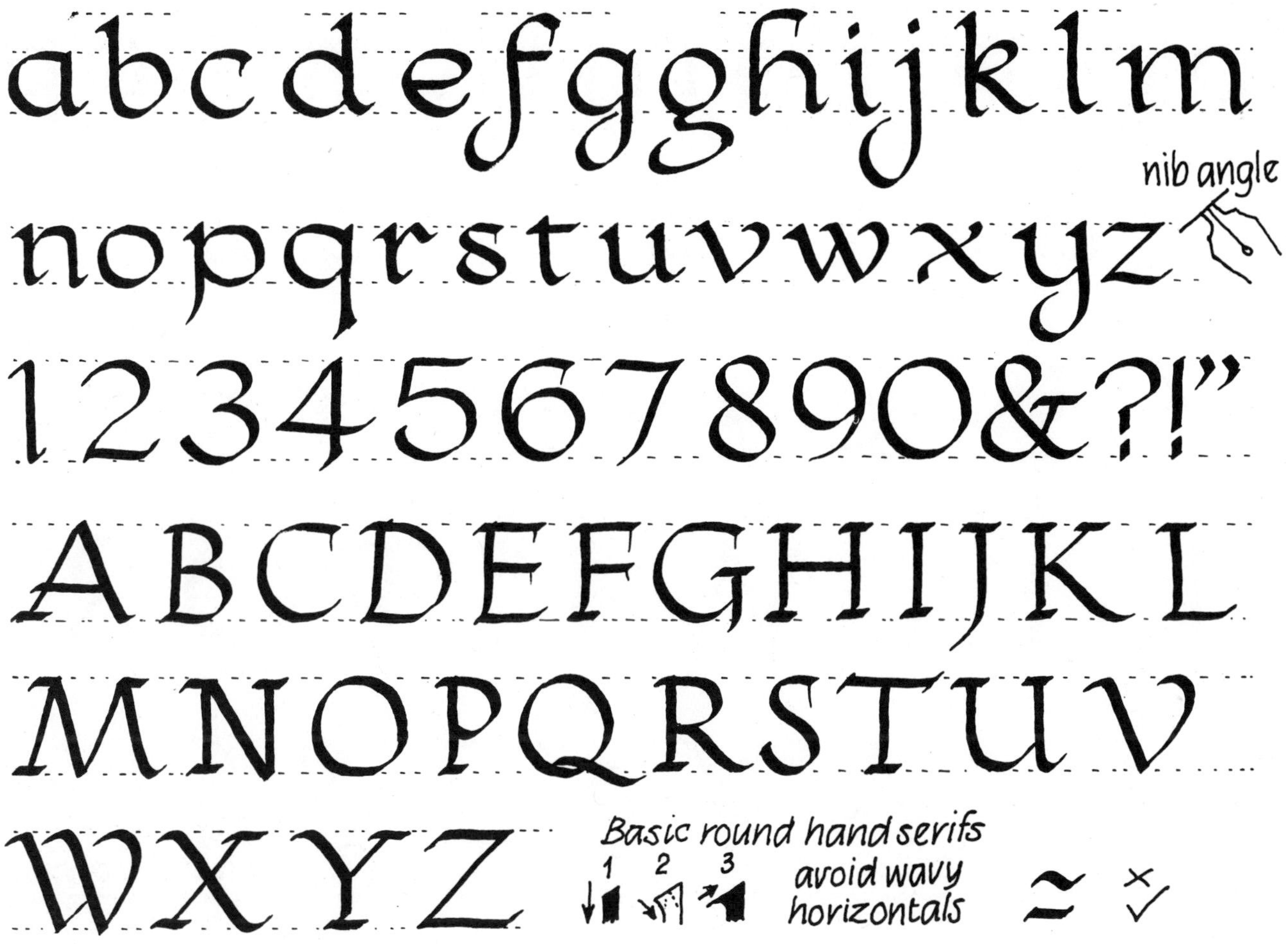

abcdefghijklmnopq

rstuvwxyz 12345

67890 ABCDEFG

HIJKLMNOPQRS

TUVWXYZ &?!" nib angle

Template for tessellated fish, see page 49

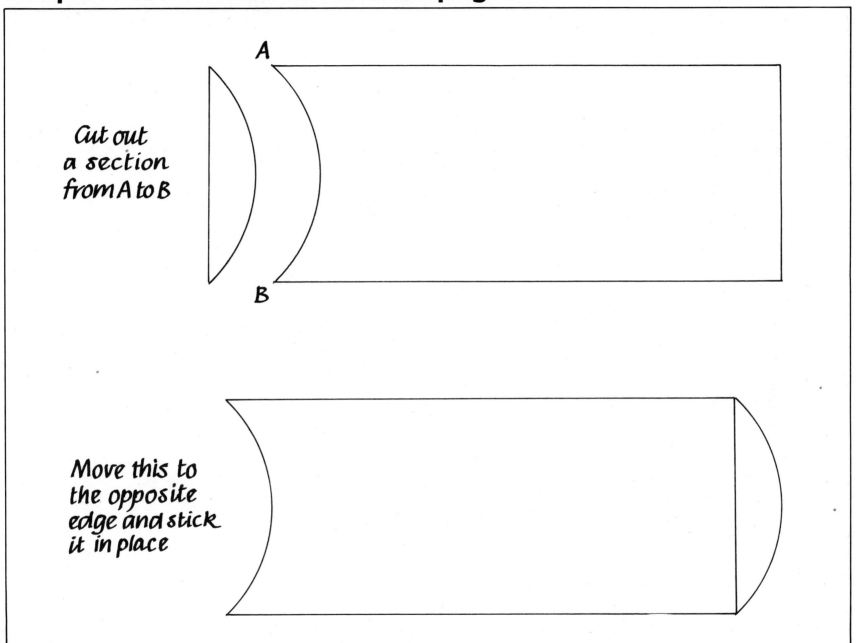

A

B

Cut out
a section
from A to B

Move this to
the opposite
edge and stick
it in place

Template for a bookmark, see page 33

This page may be photocopied for use in the classroom and should not be declared in any return in respect of any photocopying licence.

Template for a clock face and hands, see page 84

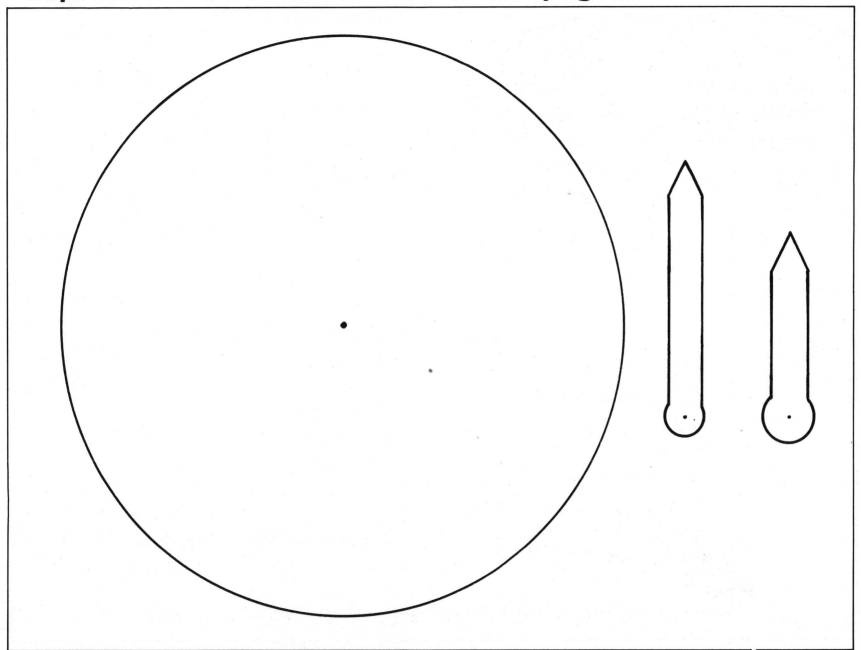

Resources

Suppliers' Addresses

Yorkshire Purchasing,
Park Lodge Lane,
Wakefield,
West Yorkshire,
WF1 4JR.
For general supplies.

Nottingham Educational Supplies,
Ludlow Hill Road,
West Bridgford,
Nottingham,
NG2 6HD.
For general supplies.

Hestair Hope Ltd,
St Philip's Drive,
Royton,
Oldham,
OL2 6AG.
For frames and mounting materials.

E J Arnold and Son Ltd,
Educational manufacturers and publishers,
Parkside Lane,
Dewsbury Road,
Leeds,
LS11 5TD.
For display materials.

Wilson and Garden Ltd,
Newton Street,
Kilsyth,
Glasgow,
G65 0JX.
For display boards.

Lawtons Ltd,
Lawco House,
60 Vauxhall Road,
Liverpool,
L69 3AU.
For storage equipment.

Daler-Rowney Ltd,
PO Box 10,
Bracknell,
Berkshire,
RG12 4ST.
For art and craft materials.

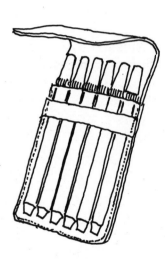

Staedtler (UK) Ltd,
Pontyclun,
Mid Glamorgan,
CF7 8YJ.
For pencils and pens.

Pictorial Charts Educational Trust,
27 Kirchen Road,
Ealing,
London,
W13 0UD.
For colourful wallcharts.

Local stationery shops,
For general supplies.

Other useful sources

You can contact large firms and industries for topic packs eg British Gas, ICI, The Post Office, Brooke Bond, Tate and Lyle, BP, The Milk Marketing Board and see *Treasure Chest for Teachers* for more addresses.

Museums often have school loan systems for artefacts, stuffed animals, prints, paintings etc. It is also possible to approach manufacturers for ends of rolls of newsprint or other paper. Printers may let you have old advertising sheets (unused but out of date) from advertising hordings. Both sides of these items can be used.

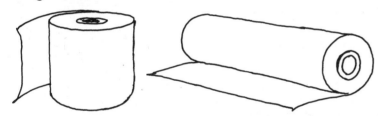

Local farms may also have some interesting pieces of old machinery which could be useful as a focal point for display. Parents often have interesting items and artefacts or they may have a skill which could be the starting point for a display or topic. Ask them for old curtains which may be used as drapes or old cotton sheets which can be dyed.

Go to your local market as well, as market traders will often find ends of cloth rolls at reasonable prices and approach upholsterers too.

Useful store cupboard items

Build up a stock of interesting objects and useful equipment for display eg cork tiles, polystyrene tiles, old vases, interesting boxes, baskets, stools, chairs, tubs, rush matting, curtains and material off-cuts. Also keep unusual natural objects such as shells, grasses, umbels, pine cones, and drift-wood.

Safety

Assuming that teachers are naturally watchful of their pupils, safety hasn't yet been mentioned with regard to display. The main point to remember is avoid siting displays near fire hazards such as electric power points, lights and heaters. For extra care you can now also buy fire retardant spray for fabrics.

Other Scholastic books

Bright Ideas

The *Bright Ideas* books provide a wealth of resources for busy primary school teachers. There are now more than 20 titles published, providing clearly explained and illustrated ideas on topics ranging from *Writing* and *Maths Activities* to *Assemblies* and *Christmas Art and Craft*. Each book contains material which can be photocopied for use in the classroom.

Teacher Handbooks

The *Teacher Handbooks* give an overview of the latest research in primary education, and show how it can be put into practice in the classroom. Covering all the core areas of the curriculum, the *Teacher Handbooks* are indispensable to the new teacher as a source of information and useful to the experienced teacher as a quick reference guide.

Management Books

The *Management Books* are designed to help teachers to organise their time, classroom and teaching more efficiently. The books deal with topical issues, such as *Parents and Schools* and organising and planning *Project Teaching*, and are written by authors with lots of practical advice and experiences to share.

Let's Investigate

Let's Investigate is an exciting range of photocopiable maths activity books giving open-ended investigative tasks. The series will complement and extend any existing maths programme. Designed to cover the 6 to 12-year-old range these books are ideal for small group or individual work. Each book presents progressively more difficult concepts and many of the activities can be adapted for use throughout the primary school. Detailed teacher's notes outlining the objectives of each photocopiable sheet and suggesting follow-up activities have been included.